Q&A File

MENU SELECTION	DESCRIPTION
Design File	Creates a database
Add Data	Adds records to the database
Search/Update	Searches and modifies records in the database
Print	Prints records in the database
Copy	Copies a database
Remove	Deletes selected or duplicate records
Mass Update	Modifies a group of database records
Post	Sends records to another database
Utilities	Imports/exports records; backs up database; links a database to SQL; recovers damaged database

Useful Keys in Q&A File

KEY	ACTION	KEY	ACTION
Up-Arrow	Moves up one line	Enter	Moves to next field
Down-Arrow	Moves down one line	Esc	Displays the previous screen
Left-Arrow	Moves one character to the left		Exits Q&A File
Right-Arrow	Moves one character to the right	Home	Moves to beginning of line
Backspace	Erases characters to the left of cursor	Home Home	Moves to top of page
		Home Home Home	Moves to top of form
Ctrl-Right-Arrow	Moves to next word	Ctrl-Home	Moves to first character of form
Ctrl-Left-Arrow	Moves to previous word	PgDn	Moves to next screen in Help
Del	Erases characters to the right of cursor		Moves to first character of next page in a form
End	Moves to end of line	PgUp	Moves to previous screen in Help
End End	Moves to end of page		
End End End	Moves to bottom of form		Moves to first character of previous page in a form
Ctrl-End	Moves to last character of form		
Enter	Continues to next screen	Tab	Moves to next field
	Enters information	Shift-Tab	Moves to previous field

Computer users are not all alike.
Neither are SYBEX books.

We know our customers have a variety of needs. They've told us so. And because we've listened, we've developed several distinct types of books to meet the needs of each of our customers. What are you looking for in computer help?

If you're looking for the basics, try the **ABC's** series. You'll find short, unintimidating tutorials and helpful illustrations. For a more visual approach, select **Teach Yourself**, featuring screen-by-screen illustrations of how to use your latest software purchase.

Mastering and **Understanding** titles offer you a step-by-step introduction, plus an in-depth examination of intermediate-level features, to use as you progress.

Our **Up & Running** series is designed for computer-literate consumers who want a no-nonsense overview of new programs. Just 20 basic lessons, and you're on your way.

We also publish two types of reference books. Our **Instant References** provide quick access to each of a program's commands and functions. SYBEX **Encyclopedias** provide a *comprehensive reference* and explanation of all of the commands, features and functions of the subject software.

Sometimes a subject requires a special treatment that our standard series doesn't provide. So you'll find we have titles like **Advanced Techniques, Handbooks, Tips & Tricks**, and others that are specifically tailored to satisfy a unique need.

We carefully select our authors for their in-depth understanding of the software they're writing about, as well as their ability to write clearly and communicate effectively. Each manuscript is thoroughly reviewed by our technical staff to ensure its complete accuracy. Our production department makes sure it's easy to use. All of this adds up to the highest quality books available, consistently appearing on best-seller charts worldwide.

You'll find SYBEX publishes a variety of books on every popular software package. Looking for computer help? Help Yourself to SYBEX.

For a complete catalog of our publications:

SYBEX Inc.

2021 Challenger Drive, Alameda, CA 94501
Tel: (415) 523-8233/(800) 227-2346 Telex: 336311
SYBEX Fax: (415) 523-2373

The
ABC's
of
Q&A 4

The
ABC's
of
Q&A™ 4

Trudi Reisner

SYBEX®

San Francisco • Paris • Düsseldorf • Soest

Acquisitions Editor: David Clark
Developmental Editor: Christian Crumlish
Editor: Kayla Sussell
Technical Editor: Nancy Dannenberg
Word Processors: Susan Trybull and Ann Dunn
Book Designer: Suzanne Albertson
Chapter Art and Layout: Lisa Jaffe
Screen Graphics: Cuong Le
Typesetter: Stephanie Hollier
Proofreader: Bill Cassel
Indexer:Ruthanne Lowe
Cover Designer: Ingalls + Associates
Cover Photographer: Michael Lamott

Library of Congress Card Number: 91-65591
ISBN: 0-89588-824-6

Manufactured in the United States of America
10 9 8 7 6 5 4 3 2 1

To
Robert L. Jones, III
in appreciation
of his encouragement
and support

ACKNOWLEDGMENTS

I want to give special thanks to Kayla Sussell, Senior Editor at Sybex, for her ability to inspire a writer to do her best.

Thanks also to Beth Nagengast, marketing manager of Symantec, for providing copies of the documentation and the software that I needed to write this book.

CONTENTS AT A GLANCE

TABLE
OF
CONTENTS

INTRODUCTION

Q&A Release 4.0, by Symantec, is an integrated software package containing four programs. Q&A Write is a word processing program used to create, edit, and print all sorts of documents. Q&A File is a database manager program used for storing and retrieving information. Q&A Report is a report generator program used to create and print professional-looking reports, and the Assistant is an artificial intelligence program, designed especially for the beginner. The Assistant lets you find and retrieve specific information with English questions instead of having to use Q&A commands.

Because Q&A's versatility encourages both business and home use, and the four programs are so easy to run, earlier releases of Q&A became popular very quickly. The latest version, Q&A Release 4.0, was distributed in May 1991. It contains many new, easy-to-use features and enhancements that are more powerful than ever before.

What This Book Is About

This book provides step-by-step instructions and practical examples to master the basics of the four different programs. It offers mini-lessons to (1) help you produce business and form letters, (2) create a database file to track information, and (3) create and print mailing labels. There are shortcuts, tips, and hints sprinkled throughout to help you get up and running, and to prevent some of the more common mistakes that you might make along the way.

Part One, "Getting Started," examines Q&A's capabilities: It demonstrates how to start the program, introduces you to Q&A's Main Menu, explains how to use the keyboard and the mouse to select menu commands, explores the on-line Help feature, and shows you how to exit Q&A.

Part Two, "Q&A Write," teaches you everything you need to know about Q&A's word processing program. You will learn how to create a business letter from start to finish.

Part Three, "Q&A File," shows you how to work with database files, and how to print form letters and envelopes.

Part Four, "Q&A Report," teaches you how to create and print professional-quality reports.

Part Five, "The Assistant," demonstrates how to work with the Assistant. It teaches you how to set up questions using the English language to find and retrieve information in Q&A database files.

Part Six, "Macros," instructs you on how to create and use macros to save time and keystrokes. When you use a macro, you can store and activate many commands by pressing only one or two keys instead of having to enter a series of commands and keystrokes.

The Appendix contains instructions for installing Q&A. It is provided especially for Q&A users who may need extra help setting up Q&A.

Who Should Read This Book

If you are new to Q&A and feel somewhat intimidated by computer programs in general, this book will help you to master the basics quickly. If you have already made an attempt to learn Q&A on your own, you might have found it difficult to learn a computer program and to be productive at the same time. This book teaches you how to run the four programs by showing you a variety of ways to produce materials that are directly related to real-life needs. *The ABC's of Q&A 4* gives you all of the basic information you need to master one of the easiest and most powerful integrated programs available today.

If you are an experienced Q&A user and want to learn about the new features in Release 4.0, you can find that information here, too. Q&A's new features and enhancements are discussed at the end of this Introduction in the section "A Look at Q&A Release 4.0" and, where appropriate, in each of the six Parts of this book.

How to Use This Book

You do not have to start at the beginning and read through to the end. You can choose the feature that you want "hands-on" practice with, and then read the appropriate corresponding lesson. For example, if you want to know how to design a database file, read Part Three, "Q&A File."

If you are an experienced Q&A user, you will find that there are many useful shortcuts, tips, and hints scattered throughout the book, and you may want to read it from the beginning to the end. Or, you may want to quickly skim through the basic material presented in Parts One through Four and then jump right into Part Five, "The Assistant," or Part Six, "Macros."

Hardware Requirements

The ABC's of Q&A 4 was written for IBM PCs and PC compatibles. Q&A Release 4.0 is available in 5-1/4 inch or 3-1/2 inch disks. It requires MS-DOS 2.1 or higher and 512K of memory. You should have a graphics card and monitor, and you will need a printer to print your documents and reports. A mouse is handy, but not necessary. You will also need formatted disks for backing up the files that you create in Q&A. Instructions on formatting disks are provided in the Appendix.

A Look at Q&A Release 4.0

There are several new features in Q&A 4.0. Mouse support is one new overall feature that encompasses all four programs. Now you can select commands from menus and navigate through fields and forms with a mouse.

New features in Q&A Write include a 660,000-word built-in thesaurus that you can use to look up synonyms to find better words for your letters and other documents. You can now enhance your documents with scalable fonts and assign a pitch size to any font you use. The new Document Switching feature in Q&A Write lets you switch from your current document to a document previously opened in that session. For easier file identification, you can now add a detailed description to the file name of a document or a database by using the new List Manager feature. And finally, Q&A Write now lets you look at your document on the screen, before you print it, with the Page Preview feature.

The new Field Template feature in Q&A File lets you set up a special field for entering information with special characters, such as parentheses or hyphens. This allows you to enter items like phone numbers and social security numbers without having to type the special characters. Q&A File will enter them for you automatically. And, you can now edit your records while in the Table view when you are working in Q&A.

One of the most important new features in Q&A Report is the Report Preview that lets you examine your report on the screen before you print it. That way, you can make any last minute changes before printing a final copy. Also, when you are in Q&A Report, you can now create cross tab reports and calculate columns and rows of numbers. Furthermore, you can now enhance text with boldface, italics, underline, superscript, subscript, strikeout, and various fonts, and you can double-space your reports.

The greatest strength of the Assistant in Release 4.0 is the new Query Guide. It assists you in building accurate English requests to retrieve, sort, and update records, to perform calculations, and to generate reports. You simply choose sentence fragments from menus to build your requests, and you can then interact with your computer through the medium of the English language.

Q&A's capability to run macros from a list, instead of requiring the user to press macro keys and type macro names, is also a new feature that makes this program even easier to run than earlier versions.

PART

ONE

Getting Started

What Can Q&A Do?

FEATURING
   Q&A Write
   Q&A File
   Q&A Report
   The Assistant

Q&A CONTAINS FOUR DIFFERENT PROGRAMS: Q&A WRITE, Q&A File, Q&A Report, and the Assistant.

Q&A Write is an easy to use word processing program used to create, edit, and print professional looking documents. You can create a document, edit your work on the screen, and then print the document with either a dot matrix or laser printer.

With Q&A Write you can prepare documents such as:

- Letters

- Memos

- Mass mailings

- Annual reports

- Tables

- Policy and training manuals

- Books

- Formal contracts

- Proposals

Q&A File is a database manager program that lets you store and retrieve information. You can create a database file, enter data in that file, sort the information to organize your work, search for specific information, and update the information quickly and easily.

With Q&A File you can prepare such database files as:

- Customer lists

- Fortune 500 lists

- Contact lists

- Logs

- Current projects

- Personnel records

- Medical records

- Insurance records

- Quality assurance records

- General ledger

Q&A Report is a report generator program that allows you to create and print reports based on information stored in a database file. You can calculate numbers in columns and rows, enhance the appearance of text with various fonts and typefaces, and print professional-quality reports.

With Q&A Report you can prepare such reports as:

- Customer reports

- Fortune 500 reports

- Sales contact reports

- Leads analysis reports

- Salary reports

- Quality assurance reports
- General ledger reports

With the Assistant you can retrieve records, sort records, update records, and create reports based on information from your Q&A File database, rather than use Q&A File and Q&A Report commands.

Starting Q&A

FEATURING
Startup

IF YOU'RE NEW TO Q&A, YOU SHOULD TAKE THE TIME TO read the Appendix at the back of this book on installing Q&A. Note that Q&A does not run on a computer without a hard disk. If you only have two floppy disk drives, it will not work.

If Q&A was installed on your computer with its standard installation procedure, the program will be stored on the hard disk that is referred to as C, in a directory called "QA."

*H*ow to Start Q&A

Let's begin working with Q&A by starting the program.

① With Drive A empty, turn your computer on. The C: > prompt appears on the screen.

② Type **cd\qa** and press Enter to change to the Q&A program.

③ At the DOS prompt, C:\QA >, type **qa**.

④ Press Enter. After a moment, Q&A loads into the memory of your computer. A title screen with the Q&A logo appears, then vanishes, and the next screen you see contains the Q&A Main Menu. Now you're ready to begin working with Q&A.

Examining Q&A's Main Menu

FEATURING

Q&A's Main Menu options

Q&A IS A "MENU DRIVEN" PROGRAM. THIS MEANS THAT you can access virtually any Q&A feature by making selections from a series of menus. See Figure 3.1 for a picture of the Main Menu.

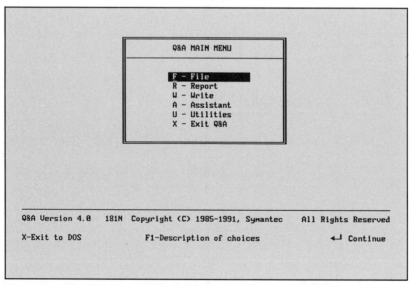

Figure 3.1: The Q&A Main Menu

There are six options listed on the Main Menu. Notice that the File option is listed first. This is convenient because initially you will probably use the Q&A File program more often than the other Q&A programs.

The Main Menu options are summarized as follows:

File   Accesses the Q&A File program; lets you create database files where you store and retrieve information.

Report   Accesses the Q&A Report program; lets you create and print reports based on the information stored in database files.

Write   Accesses the Q&A Write word processing program; allows you to write and edit letters, memos, reports, and many other types of documents.

Assistant   Accesses the Assistant; lets you find and retrieve specific information in a database file using an English-like language instead of Q&A commands.

Utilities   Accesses the Utilities program; allows you to set up your printer and change the original settings for several Q&A options.

Exit   Exits Q&A and returns you to DOS.
Q&A

Below the Q&A Main Menu you will see the key assignment line. This is a line displaying three special keys that perform specific functions to help you use the Q&A Main Menu: X-Exit to DOS, F1-Description of Choices, and ◄— Continue. "X-Exit to DOS" reminds you that you press X to exit Q&A and return to DOS. "F1-Description of Choices" gives you helpful information about the Main Menu options. When you press F1, a brief description of each Main Menu option appears on the screen. "◄— Continue" reminds you to press the Enter key to see the next screen in the program.

Using the Keyboard

FEATURING
The Enter Key
The Escape (Esc) key

YOU CHOOSE AN OPTION FROM A Q&A MENU TO PROCESS a command. You can choose commands from any menu in Q&A with the keyboard. A command on a menu that is highlighted (or in a different color) indicates that the command is current or active. As you can see in Figure 3.1, the first command, "File," is highlighted.

Q&A offers two ways to select commands from menus using the keyboard. You can use the arrow keys to highlight the command you want and then press Enter. Or, you can press the letter indicated to the left of the command on the menu to highlight the option you want and then press Enter. For the purposes of this book, let's use the second method because it takes fewer keystrokes and thus is faster.

*H*ow to Choose Commands Using the Keyboard

Follow the steps in the lesson below and you will see how easy it is to choose commands with the keyboard in Q&A.

① Press W to move the highlight to the Write option.

② Press the Enter key. This loads the Q&A Write program into your computer's memory.

③ Press the Escape (Esc) key. This key exits the current menu and returns you to the previous menu. The Main Menu reappears on your screen.

④ Press U to move the highlight to the Utilities option.

⑤ Press the Enter key. This loads the Utilities program into your computer's memory.

⑥ Press the Esc key. The Main Menu reappears.

⑦ Leave the highlight on the File option and press Enter. This loads the Q&A File program into your computer's memory.

⑧ Press the Esc key and you are returned to the Main Menu.

LESSON 5

Using the Mouse

FEATURING
The Mouse
Clicking

THE MOUSE IS A HAND-OPERATED POINTING DEVICE attached to a long cable, with two or three buttons on it. Q&A uses only the leftmost button.

If you have a mouse, and your mouse software is loaded, a mouse pointer in the shape of a rectangle appears on the screen. To move the mouse pointer, you move the mouse across the desktop or mouse pad.

There are several fundamental actions for using the mouse: (a)*pointing*—you move the mouse pointer to a specific area on the screen; (b)*clicking*—you quickly press and release the left mouse button; (c)*double-clicking*—you quickly press and release the left mouse button twice in succession; (d)*dragging*—you hold down a button while you drag something on the screen to another place on the screen; and (e)*release*—you release the button after dragging.

You can use the mouse to select commands from any Q&A menu as well for moving the cursor around. The mouse can be used instead of the cursor movement keys, the Enter key, and the Esc key.

How to Use the Mouse to Select Commands

In this book you will be shown how to use the keyboard. This is the only section that discusses how to use the mouse. If you prefer to use the mouse with Q&A, refer back to this section for instructions.

① With the mouse, move the pointer to the Write option.

② Click the left mouse button and then release it. This selects the Write option and loads the Q&A Write program into your computer's memory.

③ Click the left mouse button anywhere outside the Q&A Write menu. This exits the current menu and returns you to the previous menu. The Main Menu reappears on the screen. Clicking the left mouse button anywhere *outside* a menu performs the same function as pressing the Esc key to exit a menu. This does *not* work with the Q&A Main Menu, however, to exit the Q&A Main Menu, you must press X. You cannot use the mouse to exit the Q&A program.

④ Move the pointer to the Utilities option.

⑤ Click the left mouse button and then release it. This loads the Utilities program into your computer's memory.

⑥ Click the left mouse button anywhere outside the Q&A Utilities menu. The Main Menu reappears.

⑦ Move the pointer to the File option.

⑧ Click the left mouse button and then release it. This loads the Q&A File program into your computer's memory.

⑨ Click the left mouse button anywhere outside the Q&A File menu and you are returned to the Q&A Main Menu.

Using On-line Help

FEATURING

The F1 (Help) function Key

THE Q&A HELP SYSTEM CONTAINS INFORMATION THAT will assist you as you learn and use Q&A. There are "pages" or Help screens for each command in Q&A. Each Help screen contains brief descriptions and shows examples of the function of each command. You can get Help information on a particular topic from anywhere in the program at any time.

You should access Help when you're about to begin a task and don't remember how to execute a command, or when you're in the middle of performing a task and you don't know how to continue. After you read the relevant Help screen, you exit Help and return to your work exactly where you left off.

When you want to get quick help on a particular function, command, or task, use the on-line Help screen. For example, suppose you want further information about the options on the Q&A Main Menu. Simply press the F1 (Help) function key, and Q&A displays a Help screen. The Help screen contains a brief description of each option on the menu.

How to Get Help Using On-line Help

To access on-line help, you can always press the F1 (Help) function key from anywhere in the program at any time. There are friendly reminders at the bottom of every screen in Q&A. You will see either "F1-Description of Choices" or "F1-Help."

① Press the F1 (Help) function key and you are presented with a Help screen that contains information about the options on the Q&A Main Menu, as shown in Figure 6.1.

② When you're finished reading the Help screen, press the Esc key. This exits Help and returns you to your original place in the program.

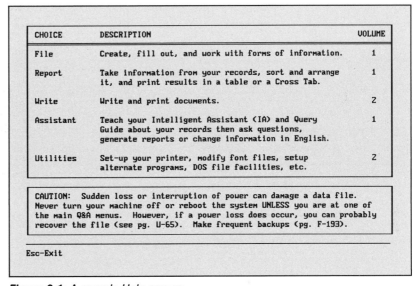

CHOICE	DESCRIPTION	VOLUME
File	Create, fill out, and work with forms of information.	1
Report	Take information from your records, sort and arrange it, and print results in a table or a Cross Tab.	1
Write	Write and print documents.	2
Assistant	Teach your Intelligent Assistant (IA) and Query Guide about your records then ask questions, generate reports or change information in English.	1
Utilities	Set-up your printer, modify font files, setup alternate programs, DOS file facilities, etc.	2

CAUTION: Sudden loss or interruption of power can damage a data file. Never turn your machine off or reboot the system UNLESS you are at one of the main Q&A menus. However, if a power loss does occur, you can probably recover the file (see pg. U-65). Make frequent backups (pg. F-193).

Esc-Exit

Figure 6.1: *A sample Help screen*

LESSON 7

Exiting Q&A

FEATURING

Exiting the program

BEFORE YOU EXIT THE Q&A PROGRAM, IT IS A GOOD idea to save the open files that you are working on. In the event of a power failure, a program crash, or some other disaster, saving your files with the Save command ensures that you won't lose any of your work. Instructions for using the Save command are provided in the appropriate sections throughout this book.

If you have made any changes to a file (even if you only press the Spacebar or the Enter key), Q&A asks you if you want to save the file before quitting the program. This reminder can be very helpful.

How to Exit Q&A and Return to DOS

Notice that the Exit Q&A option is the last item on the Main Menu. Let's see how to exit Q&A now.

① From the Main Menu, press X to move the highlight to the Exit Q&A option.

② When you do, you leave the program and you are returned to the DOS prompt, C:\QA>.

③ With the DOS prompt on the screen, you can turn off your computer.

PART

TWO

Q&A Write

Starting Q&A Write

FEATURING

The Q&A Write menu

THE FIRST STEP TOWARD USING Q&A'S WORD PROCESSING program is to start the Q&A Write program. See Part One if you need to review the startup procedure.

The startup procedures load the Q&A Write program into your computer's memory. When you see the Write menu, you are ready to create a document.

The Write menu displays the following eight options:

Type/Edit	Edits the current document.
Define Page	Specifies the page size, margins, characters per inch, starting page number, and text for headers and footers.
Print	Specifies print options and prints a hard copy of your document.
Clear	Clears the current document from memory and the screen and starts a new document.
Get	Retrieves a document from disk and makes it the current document on the screen.
Save	Saves the current document to disk.

Utilities	Changes the original settings for editing options, and importing and exporting documents.
Mailing Labels	Creates, edits, and prints mailing labels.

How to Start Q&A Write

The first menu option, Type/Edit, appears highlighted or in a different color on the screen. To select an option from the Q&A Write menu, use the arrow keys and press the Enter key.

① From the Q&A Main Menu, press W to highlight the Write option.

② Press the Enter key. The Q&A Write Menu appears on the screen, as shown in Figure 8.1.

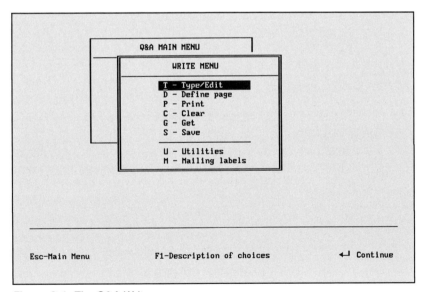

Figure 8.1: *The Q&A Write menu*

LESSON 9

Creating a New Document

FEATURING

The Type/Edit option

WITH Q&A WRITE YOU CAN CREATE ANY KIND OF document from a short memo to a novel as long as *War and Peace*. To create a document in Q&A Write enter the text, correct errors with the keyboard and/or the mouse, and then save the text in a file on disk.

Once you load Q&A Write, you can create a new document from scratch by selecting the Type/Edit option. The Type/Edit option is used when you want (1) to create a new document or (2) to edit an existing document.

When you select Type/Edit you will see a blank screen. This is where you will enter your document. A Ruler line, a Status line, and a key assignment line are at the bottom of the screen. See Figure 9.1.

The Ruler line displays tab stops and margins. The Status line displays either the name of the document, or "Working Copy" if the document hasn't been named and saved. It also shows the amount of memory used. For example, 0% means the document is empty or has very few characters in it. The Status line also displays the current position of the cursor on the screen. The key assignment line displays Q&A Write's word processing functions with their corresponding function keys.

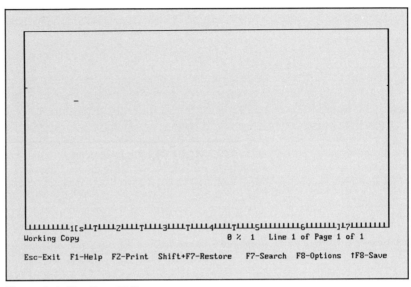

Working Copy   0 % 1   Line 1 of Page 1 of 1

Esc-Exit F1-Help F2-Print Shift+F7-Restore   F7-Search F8-Options ↑F8-Save

Figure 9.1: *The Type/Edit screen*

How to Create a New Document

Follow the steps in the lessons in Part Two to write, change, and print a typical business letter and to acquire some experience with Q&A Write. Once you complete the lessons, you will understand how to create simple documents with Q&A Write, and you will be ready to start writing letters of your own. Let's try it now.

① The Type/Edit option in the Q&A Write menu should be highlighted. If it isn't, press T to highlight Type/Edit now.

② To start a new document, press the Enter key.

LESSON 10

Entering Text

FEATURING

The Enter key
The Backspace key

WHEN YOU ENTER Q&A WRITE'S TYPE/EDIT SCREEN, an empty screen is displayed. Q&A Write automatically positions the cursor, a blinking horizontal line, at the top of the screen where you will enter text. To enter text, just start typing. Do not press the Enter key at the end of every line. The word wrap feature automatically wraps the text down to the next line.

You *do* use the Enter key when you want to control the length of particular lines. For example, use the Enter key to end paragraphs, or for short lines such as in lists or short headings, and also to indicate a blank line.

When typing, don't be concerned about making errors. Correcting typing errors is a simple task with Q&A Write. If you do catch a mistake while typing, you can use the Backspace key, usually located in the upper-right corner of your keyboard, to erase the error. Pressing the backspace key erases one character to the immediate left of the cursor. Then retype the text. For the purposes of this lesson, the Backspace key should be sufficient to help you correct minor errors, however, you will be shown how to make other corrections in Lesson 14.

To give these lessons some context, let's suppose throughout Part Two that you're working for a commercial interior design company, called Office Designs. A major account called Kase Express has recently made a large purchase from Office Designs. The chief purchasing agent has requested a volume discount and you must write a letter to discuss the discount.

How to Enter Text in a Document

The business letter you are going to type into the document will take up two screens. With the basic information about entering text that you now have, it is time to create your first letter.

① Type today's date and press Enter five times.

② Type **Ms. Gail Kase** and press Enter.

③ Type **Kase Express** and press Enter.

④ Type **384 Silas Marner Parkway** and press Enter.

⑤ Type **Brooklyn, New York**. Press the Spacebar twice. Then type **01090** and press Enter. You have now completed the inside address for your letter.

⑥ Press Enter again to leave a blank line of space between the inside address and the salutation.

⑦ Type **Dear Ms. Kase:** and press Enter twice. You have now entered the salutation for your letter. (Pressing Enter the first time ends the short line and pressing Enter the second time leaves a blank line of space between the salutation and the first line of your letter.)

⑧ To enter the first paragraph of your letter, type

> **In the May 1991 meeting with you at Kase Express, the primary topic of discussion was pricing on our office components. Dana Smith, your chief purchasing agent, felt that more favorable pricing should be given to Kase Express, given the size of purchases in previous contracts.**

⑨ Press Enter twice. Your letter should now look like the letter shown in Figure 10.1.

<u>10</u>   To enter the second paragraph of your letter, type,

We settled on a compromise arrangement, in which our pricing would be reduced 10%, provided Kase Express increased its purchases to 150 office components this year versus its previous 100 last year. We would like to present this proposal to you this month. We will contact you this week to set up a time to meet. Thank you for your time.

<u>11</u>   Press Enter twice.

<u>12</u>   Type **Sincerely,** and press Enter five times to add blank lines for a signature.

<u>13</u>   Type your name and press Enter.

<u>14</u>   Type **Director of Marketing** and press Enter. You have now completed the letter. Compare your letter to the letter shown in Figure 10.2.

<u>15</u>   Now, proceed to Lesson 11 to learn how to save this document.

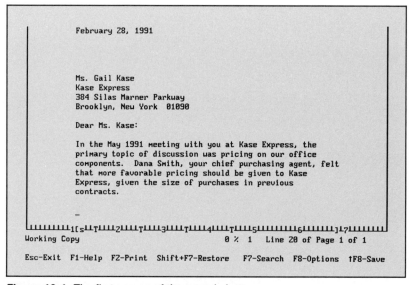

Figure 10.1: The first screen of the sample letter

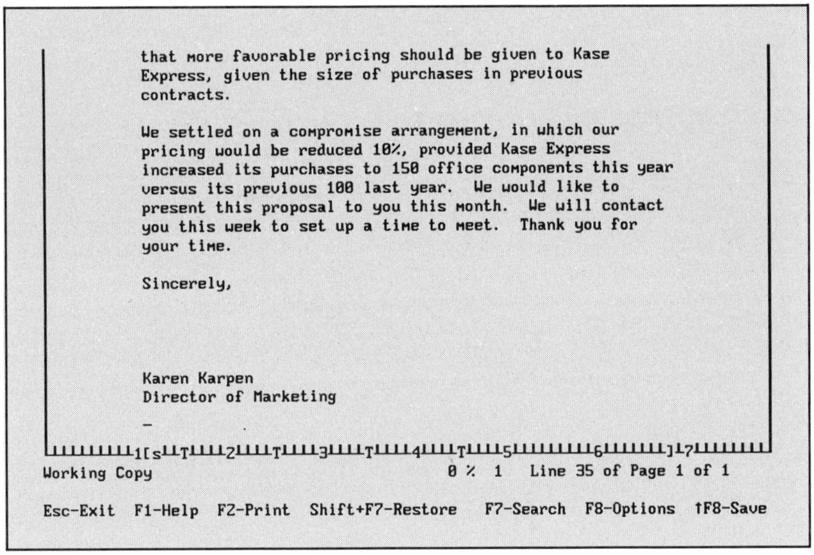

```
           that more favorable pricing should be given to Kase
           Express, given the size of purchases in previous
           contracts.

           We settled on a compromise arrangement, in which our
           pricing would be reduced 10%, provided Kase Express
           increased its purchases to 150 office components this year
           versus its previous 100 last year.  We would like to
           present this proposal to you this month.  We will contact
           you this week to set up a time to meet.  Thank you for
           your time.

           Sincerely,




           Karen Karpen
           Director of Marketing
           _
  ⊥⊥⊥⊥⊥⊥⊥⊥⊥1[s⊥⊥⊤⊥⊥⊥⊥2⊥⊥⊥⊤⊥⊥⊥⊥3⊥⊥⊥⊤⊥⊥⊥⊥4⊥⊥⊥⊤⊥⊥⊥⊥5⊥⊥⊥⊥⊥⊥⊥⊥⊥6⊥⊥⊥⊥⊥⊥⊥]⊥7⊥⊥⊥⊥⊥⊥⊥
  Working Copy                              0 %  1   Line 35 of Page 1 of 1

  Esc-Exit  F1-Help  F2-Print  Shift+F7-Restore   F7-Search  F8-Options  ↑F8-Save
```

Figure 10.2: *The second screen of the sample letter*

Saving a Document

FEATURING

The Shift-F8 (Save) function key
The Clear option

THE TEXT YOU ENTER INTO A NEW DOCUMENT IS HELD temporarily in the computer's memory. To retain this information permanently, you save your document by giving it a file name and storing the document on disk.

Q&A Write automatically assigns a temporary file name called "Working Copy" for every new document. It appears on the Status line at the bottom of the screen. Seeing the name as "Working Copy" is a clue that you have never saved the document before. You can work on the document with its temporary name until you save the document and then you give it a name.

When you give the new file a name, the temporary file name is replaced with the new file name.

How to Save a Document

There is a safety feature built into Q&A for saving a file. When you try to exit the program without first saving the file to disk, Q&A automatically asks you if you want to save the file before exiting the program. At this point, you can choose to save the file or to continue with the exit procedure without saving any changes you made to the document.

Remember, if you choose not to save the document, the text will be lost forever.

So far you have not saved the document. Let's save the document now before going any further.

① From the Type/Edit screen, hold down the Shift key and press the F8 (Save) function key. The Save screen appears, as shown in Figure 11.1.

② Q&A Write file names can have one to eight characters with letters, numbers, or a combination of both. Do not use spaces and punctuation such as periods, commas, or colons within the file name. A good tip to remember when naming files is to enter a file name that describes the content of the document in abbreviated form and lists the revision number. For example, KASELTR describes the document's content as the letter to Kase. If it is the first draft, you can add the number 1. The complete file name is KASELTR1. Type **kaseltr1**.

③ Press Enter. You are returned to the Type/Edit screen. Notice the file name "KASELTR1" replaced "Working Copy" in the Status line at the bottom of the screen.

You have now saved your document.

In the event of a power failure, a system problem, or an accident, *i.e.*, someone accidentally kicks the plug out from your computer, you could lose all of the data you have entered. To avoid losing work, save your document at least every 15 minutes. Saving a document at regular intervals ensures that the information you have entered since the last time you saved your document is safe and stored on disk. Otherwise that information is lost.

The more often you save, the smaller the amount of text that could be lost because of a power interruption. That translates into much less work that you would have to redo.

When you've finished working on a document, and you have saved it, you can clear the screen by using the Clear command.

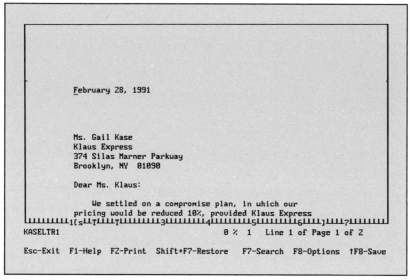

February 28, 1991

Ms. Gail Kase
Klaus Express
374 Silas Marner Parkway
Brooklyn, NY 01090

Dear Ms. Klaus:

We settled on a compromise plan, in which our
pricing would be reduced 10%, provided Klaus Express

KASELTR1   0 % 1   Line 1 of Page 1 of 2

Esc-Exit F1-Help F2-Print Shift+F7-Restore   F7-Search F8-Options ↑F8-Save

Figure 11.1: The saved document

How to Clear the Screen

Let's clear the screen now and see how the Clear command works.

① Press Esc to exit the Type/Edit screen. You are returned to the Q&A Write menu.

② Press C to move the highlight to the Clear option.

③ Press Enter.

④ Leave the highlight on the Type/Edit option and press Enter. Notice the screen is blank, ready for you to start working with a new document. The message "New document" appears in the bottom left corner of the screen.

⑤ Press Esc to exit to the Q&A Write menu.

The Get Option

FEATURING

Retrieving documents

WHEN YOU WANT TO RETRIEVE AN EXISTING DOCUMENT file and you know the name of the file, you can use the Get command from the Q&A Write menu. If you don't remember the name of the file you want to retrieve, you can ask Q&A Write to list the documents that you have saved.

You can retrieve existing documents from Q&A Write in two ways. You can get a document when you start the Q&A Write program and you want to work in the Type/Edit screen. Or, after saving a document, you can clear the screen with the Clear command, discussed in Lesson 11, and either start a new document or load any document that you have saved.

*H*ow to Retrieve a Document You Saved

Let's retrieve the letter you saved earlier.

1. From the Q&A Write menu, press G to move the highlight to the Get option.

2. Press Enter. A dialog box appears. The default drive and directory, C:\QA appear in the dialog box.

③ Because you know the name of the document is KASELTR1, you could type it now, but let's take a look at the list of documents saved. When you don't know the exact name of a document, you can ask Q&A Write to list the existing documents. Press Enter.

④ Find your document in the list and move the highlight to it. Press Enter. You are presented with the letter you typed in the Type/Edit screen.

Moving around in a Document

USUALLY, DOCUMENTS HAVE MORE TEXT THAN CAN FIT on one screen. You can navigate through your document to bring different parts of it into view.

The Status Line

The Status line at the bottom of the screen indicates the current position of the cursor. It shows the current column position, the current line number, the current page number, and the total number of pages in the document. As you move the cursor in your document, the cursor position changes in the Status line.

The Status line can be compared to the rear view mirror in a car. When you look in your rear view mirror, you check where your car is on the road in relation to the other cars. When learning how to use Q&A Write, you should check the Status line frequently to see where your cursor is positioned in your document.

The Status line is very handy when you're working on a document because it tells you where you can begin typing and where you can begin a word processing task. For example, if you want to correct an error in Position 12, Line 1 of your document, you move your cursor to that location, check the Status line to see the current cursor position, and then perform the task.

*T*he Arrow Keys

The arrow keys are located on the far right side of your keyboard. When you continue to hold down any of the arrow keys you will find that they are repeating keys. This means that continuous pressing of an arrow key moves the cursor quickly in the indicated direction repeatedly.

The Right-Arrow and Left-Arrow keys move the cursor horizontally. If you want to move the cursor when you are not typing, press the Right-Arrow key to move it to the right one character at a time. Press the Left-Arrow key to move it to the left one character at a time. If you want to move the cursor vertically, you press the Up-Arrow and Down-Arrow keys. They move the cursor up and down one line at a time.

You can use the arrow keys alone or in combination with other keys. Using the arrow keys alone works fine, but when moving larger distances, it can quickly become tedious.

Fortunately, there are faster ways to move around the document, using the Home and End keys in conjunction with the arrow keys and the Ctrl key. You can also use the PgUp and PgDn keys. All of the cursor movement keys are summarized in the following list.

Right-Arrow	Moves the cursor to the right one character at a time.
Left-Arrow	Moves the cursor to the left one character at a time.
Up-Arrow	Moves the cursor up one line at a time.
Down-Arrow	Moves the cursor down one line at a time.

Ctrl + Right-Arrow	Moves the cursor right one word at a time.
Ctrl + Left-Arrow	Moves the cursor left one word at a time.
Home	Moves the cursor to the beginning of a line.
End	Moves the cursor to the end of a line.
PgDn	Moves the cursor down one full screen at a time.
PgUp	Moves the cursor up one full screen at a time.
Ctrl + Home	Moves the cursor to the top of the document.
Ctrl + End	Moves the cursor to the bottom of the document.
Ctrl + F7 (Go To)	Moves the cursor to a specific page in the document.

Suppose you are working on a document that contains multiple pages and you know which page you want to move to. How can you move to a specific page quickly? Use the Ctrl + F7 (Go To) key. For example, to move to page 2, you hold down the Ctrl key and press F7. Q&A Write asks you to enter the number of the page you want. You type **2** and then press F10. This takes you to page 2 instantly.

How to Move Around the Document

Now let's explore how to move around the document with Q&A Write's cursor movement keys.

① Using the Up-Arrow key, move the cursor to line 1 in your document by pressing the key to move the cursor up, one line at a time. Notice that as the cursor moves up through the document, one line at a time, the text on the bottom disappears. Notice also that the position and line number in the Status line changes to reflect the current position of the cursor as it moves up the screen.

② Holding down the Down-Arrow key instead of just pressing it, move the cursor to the last line in your document. Notice the cursor quickly moves down to line 34. Check the line number in the Status line to verify this.

③ Using the Up-Arrow key, move the cursor to the first paragraph, position 1, line 13. Be sure to verify the cursor position by looking at the position and line number in the Status line.

④ Holding down the Right-Arrow key instead of just pressing it, move the cursor to the right one character at a time, until it is at the right edge on the screen.

⑤ Holding down the Left-Arrow key instead of pressing it, move the cursor to the left one character at a time, until it is at the left edge on the screen.

⑥ Hold down the Ctrl key, usually located near the Spacebar on your keyboard, and press the Right-Arrow key until the cursor is on the last word in the line. Notice the cursor moves to the right to the beginning of each word. This feature is especially handy when you want to insert or delete words.

⑦ Hold down the Ctrl key, and press the Left-Arrow key until the cursor is on the first word in the line. Notice the cursor moves to the left to the beginning of each word.

⑧ Press the End key, usually located above the arrow keys on your keyboard. Notice the cursor moves quickly to the end of the line.

⑨ Press the Home key, usually located above the End key on your keyboard. As you may have guessed, the cursor moves quickly to the beginning of the line.

⑩ Press the PgDn key, usually located to the right of the End key on your keyboard. Notice the cursor moves quickly down one full screen. The text in the top portion of the screen slides up and you can now see only the closing in the bottom portion of your letter.

⑪ Press the PgUp key, usually located to the right of the Home key on your keyboard. Notice the cursor moves quickly up one full screen. The text in the bottom portion of the screen slides down and you can now see only the top portion of your letter.

⑫ Hold down the Ctrl key and press the End key. Notice the cursor moves quickly down to the last line, line 34, at the bottom of your document.

⑬ Hold down the Ctrl key and press the Home key. Notice the cursor moves quickly up to the first line, position 1 at the top of your document.

Correcting Mistakes

FEATURING

Overtype mode

YOU HAVE LEARNED HOW TO CORRECT TYPING MISTAKES *while* entering text by using the Backspace key to erase incorrect characters or words and then retyping the corrected text. But how do you correct mistakes *after* the text has been entered in a document? Fortunately, Q&A Write lets us edit existing text with Overtype mode.

In Q&A Write there are two text entry modes—Overtype and Insert. When editing text, you can either type over existing text or insert new text. Q&A Write is set to Overtype mode when you first start. This means that you can change text or correct minor errors simply by typing the new text over the existing text.

For example, suppose that the letter you wrote in Lesson 10 is incorrectly addressed. The street number in the address line should be 374 and not "384." Suppose further that the number of office components in the second paragraph should be 125 and not "150." Furthermore, you want to change the word "like" in the second paragraph to "want."

How to Correct Mistakes Using Overtype Mode

Let's use Overtype mode now to make these corrections.

(1) Use the Down-Arrow and Right-Arrow keys to position the cursor on the "8" in the street number on the address line, line 8, position 2.

(2) Type **7**. This changes the number from 384 to 374.

(3) Press the PgDn key.

(4) Press the Up-Arrow key to move the cursor to line 22.

(5) Press Ctrl-Right-Arrow four times to move the cursor to the number "150."

(6) Press the Right-Arrow key to move the cursor to the "5" in the number "150."

(7) Type **25**. This changes the number from 150 to 125.

(8) Press the Down-Arrow key to move the cursor to line 23.

(9) Press Ctrl-Right-Arrow three times to move the cursor to the word "like."

(10) Type **want**. This changes the word "like" to "want."

Inserting Text

FEATURING

The Ins (Insert) key

IN INSERT MODE YOU CAN *ADD* CHARACTERS, SPACES, or symbols to a document without changing or deleting existing text. As you enter new text, existing text to the right of the cursor automatically adjusts to accommodate the inserted text.

Because Q&A Write is normally in Overtype mode you must press the Ins (Insert) key to switch to Q&A Write's Insert mode.

After you switch to Insert mode, position the cursor where you want to insert text and then type the text. In most cases, you will be inserting text more often than you will be typing over text.

How to Insert Text

There are three insertions you will make in your letter. You will insert the word "partition" after the word "office" in the first paragraph, and you will insert the word "later" before the word "this" in the next-to-last sentence of the second paragraph. The third insertion is to add your middle initial to your name. Let's try it.

① Press Ctrl-Home. This moves the cursor to the top of the document, position 1, line 1. It is a good idea to start with the cursor at the top of the document so you can see where the cursor is located in the document before you make any changes.

② Press the Down-Arrow key to move the cursor to line 15, position 1.

③ Press the Ins key, which is usually located to the left of the Home key on your keyboard. The "Ins" indicator appears on the Status line to the left of 0% at the bottom of the screen. Notice that the cursor changes from an underline to a small square.

④ Type **partition** and press the Spacebar. You have now inserted a word followed by a space. Notice the surrounding text adjusts automatically.

⑤ Using the Down-Arrow key, move the cursor to line 24.

⑥ Press Ctrl-Right-Arrow four times to move the cursor to the word "this" just before the word "month."

⑦ Type **later** and press the Spacebar. Notice how the text surrounding the new word adjusts automatically.

⑧ Use the Down-Arrow key to move the cursor to line 33.

⑨ Hold down the Ctrl key and press the Left-Arrow to move the cursor to the first letter of your last name.

⑩ Type your middle initial and a period (.).

⑪ Press the Spacebar. Notice how your last name shifts to the right to accommodate your middle initial.

⑫ Press the Ins key to exit Insert mode. Notice the Ins indicator disappears from the Status line. The cursor changes from a small square back to the underline again.

⑬ Press Ctrl-Home to move the cursor to the top of the document again.

If you want to take a break now, press Shift-F8 to save your document. Press Enter to accept the file name KASELTER1. Press Esc to exit the Type/Edit screen, and press Esc again to exit Q&A Write. You are returned to the Q&A Main Menu.

Deleting Text

FEATURING

The Del (Delete) key
F3 (Delete Block) function key
F4 (Delete Word) function key

WITH THE DEL (DELETE) KEY YOU CAN DELETE A SINGLE character, word, sentence, paragraph, or section of text. When you want to remove a *block* of text you can use the F3 Delete Block function key. Use the cursor movement keys to highlight the text and then remove the text by pressing the F3 Delete Block function key.

How to Delete Text

If you exited Q&A Write in the previous lesson, read Lesson 12 on Retrieving Saved Documents to retrieve your letter before starting this lesson.

In your letter you will make the following changes. In the address, "New York" should be changed to "NY." In the first sentence, the word "primary" should be deleted. In the last sentence, "Thank you for your time" should be deleted. The entire second paragraph should be deleted in this lesson, and in the next lesson you will see how to restore it.

① Press the Down-Arrow key to move the cursor to line 9.

② Press Ctrl-Right-Arrow to move the cursor to the right one word. Now the cursor should be on the "N" in New York.

③ Press the Right-Arrow key to move the cursor to the "e" in "New York."

④ Press the Delete (Del) key, which is usually located below the Ins key on your keyboard, three times.

⑤ Press the Right-Arrow key once to move to the "o" in "New York."

⑥ Press the Del key three times. You have now changed "New York" to "NY."

⑦ Press the Down-Arrow key to move the cursor to line 14, position 1, to the "p" in "primary."

⑧ Press F4 to delete the word "primary." When you want to delete a word using the F4 key, be sure that the cursor is on the first character of the word. Otherwise, if you position the cursor in the middle of the word, only part of the word will be deleted.

⑨ Now let's delete a sentence. First, move the cursor to line 25.

⑩ Press the End key to move the cursor to the end of the line.

⑪ Press the Left-Arrow key to position the cursor on the period.

⑫ Press F3. The prompt, "Use the arrow keys to select the text you want to remove, then press F10" appears at the bottom of the screen.

⑬ Press the period (.) to highlight the sentence instead of using the arrow keys. This is a quick way to highlight a sentence.

⑭ Press F10 to delete the sentence. The last sentence in the second paragraph disappears.

⑮ Let's delete the second paragraph. To begin, move the cursor to line 20.

⑯   Press Home. The cursor is at the beginning of the second paragraph.

⑰   Press F3. The prompt, "Use the arrow keys to select the text you want to remove, then press F10" appears at the bottom of the screen.

⑱   Press Enter twice to highlight the paragraph and the return following the paragraph instead of using the arrow keys. This is a quick way to highlight a paragraph, and to include the spacing below the paragraph.

⑲   Press F10 to delete the paragraph. The second paragraph disappears. In the next lesson you will learn how to restore this paragraph.

Restoring Deleted Text

FEATURING

The Shift-F7 (Restore Text)
function key

WHEN WORKING ON A DOCUMENT YOU CAN SOMETIMES
erase text accidentally. Don't fret. With Q&A Write's Restore Text
command you can restore the text that you deleted. It allows you to
undo the last deletion you made with either the F3 or F4 function key.
If you press Backspace or Delete to delete text, however, the Restore
Text command will not work.

How to Restore Deleted Text

Keep in mind that you can only use the Restore Text command
immediately after the deleting action has taken place. Otherwise you
will lose the original text. If you use another delete, or copy, or move
command immediately after the deleting action, the original text is
replaced with the text from the second action.

① To restore text press the Shift-F7 (Restore Text) function key.
It's like magic! By pressing one key, the previously deleted
paragraph reappears in your document again.

② Let's delete a word and then restore it. Move the cursor
down to the third paragraph. Then move the cursor to the
"s" in the word "settled."

LESSON 17

③ Press F4 to delete the word "settled." Q&A Write removes the word and stores it in your computer's memory.

④ Press the Shift-F7 (Restore Text) function key. You have now brought back the word by pressing one key.

⑤ Let's delete a line of text and then restore it. Move the cursor to the beginning of the line that contains your name.

⑥ Press the Shift-F4 key to delete the line. Your name disappears.

⑦ Press the Shift-F7 (Restore Text) function key. You have now restored your name.

Copying Text from One Location to Another

YOU CAN DUPLICATE TEXT WITHIN A DOCUMENT OR between documents. Instead of retyping a phrase, paragraph, or several pages of text, you can copy the text, and insert it into another location.

Q&A Write provides two ways to copy text. You can copy a block of text within a document or copy a block of text to another document.

In your letter, you will be copying the second paragraph to the bottom of the document for the sake of practice.

How to Copy Text

Let's see how the Copy command works in Q&A Write.

①   Position the cursor at the beginning of the second paragraph in your letter, line 20, position 1. This is the beginning of the block of text that you will copy.

②   Press the F5 (Copy) function key. The prompt "Use the arrow keys to select the text you want to copy, then press F10" appears at the bottom of the screen.

③ Press the Enter key twice to highlight the paragraph and the
blank line of space below it as a shortcut, instead of using the
arrow keys. The text appears highlighted or in a different color
on the screen. This is the text you will be copying. Be sure to
include spacing when selecting the text you want to copy. That
way, you won't have to enter the spacing after the text is copied
to the new location. It saves you time and typing.

④ Press F10. This stores a copy of the text in your computer's
memory. The prompt "Move the cursor to the place you
want the text copied, then press F10" appears at the bottom
of the screen. Notice the paragraph appears highlighted or in
a different color on your screen.

⑤ Press the Down-Arrow key to move the cursor to line 35,
position 1. This is where you will copy the text to.

⑥ Press F10. A copy of the paragraph appears in the new location, at the bottom of the document, as shown in Figure 18.1.
The cursor returns to the beginning of the block of text that
you copied.

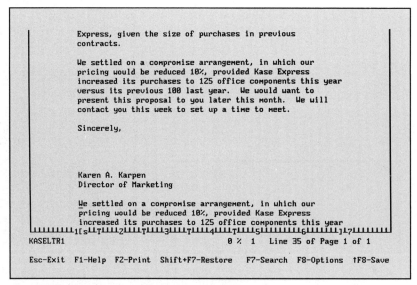

Figure 18.1: *The letter with a copied paragraph*

Moving Text from One Location to Another

FEATURING

The Shift-F5 (Move) function key

WHEN YOU MOVE TEXT, YOU REMOVE IT FROM THE original location and put it elsewhere in the document. Moving text is useful when you want to swap the order of words, lines, sentences, and paragraphs. You can also change the order of items in a list with the Move command.

How to Move Text

Just for practice, let's move the paragraph you copied in the previous lesson to the top of the letter using the Move command.

1. Leave the cursor at the beginning of the last paragraph in your letter, line 35, position 1. This is the beginning of the block of text that you will move.

2. Press the Shift-F5 (Move) function key. The prompt "Use the arrow keys to select the text you want to move, then press F10" appears at the bottom of the screen.

3. Press the Enter key twice to highlight the paragraph and the return below it. The text appears highlighted or in a different color on the screen. This is the text you will be moving. Be sure to include spacing when selecting the text you want to move.

④ Press F10. This stores the text that you want to move in your computer's memory. The prompt "Move the cursor to the place you want the text moved, then press F10" appears at the bottom of the screen. Notice the paragraph is highlighted or in a different color on your screen.

⑤ Press PgUp.

⑥ Press the Up-Arrow key to move the cursor to line 13, position 1. This is where you will move the text to.

⑦ Press F10. The paragraph appears in the new location, at the top of the document, shown in Figure 19.1. Now this paragraph is the first paragraph in the letter. Notice the return that you included at the end of the paragraph now separates the first and second paragraphs.

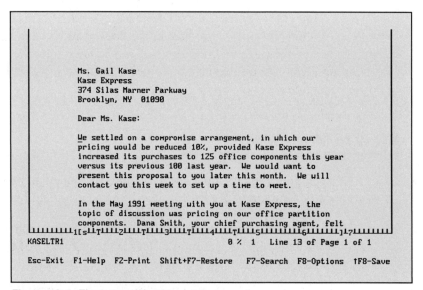

Figure 19.1: The letter with a moved paragraph

Searching for Text: Finding a Specific Word

FEATURING

The F7 (Search) function key

Q&A WRITE PROVIDES A WAY TO LOCATE SPECIFIC TEXT IN documents. You can search for text with the Search command rather than reading through the document on-screen or on hard copy to find occurrences of a particular word repeated throughout the document. Once you find the word or group of words you were searching for, you can make changes to them. The changes can be made individually or globally throughout the document with the Replace command, as will be explained later in the next section on the Replace command.

How to Search for a Specific Word in Your Document

You can use the Search command to locate the name Kase throughout the document. Once you know where each occurrence of the name is located and how many times it is used, it is easier to make changes to it.

① Press Ctrl-Home to move the cursor to the top of the document.

② Press the F7 (Search) function key. The Search dialog box appears, as shown in Figure 20.1.

③ In the "Search for" field, type **kase**. This is the word Q&A Write will search for in the document. By typing lowercase characters, Q&A Write will search for characters in both lower and uppercase.

④ Press the F7 (Search) function key. Q&A Write searches for the first occurrence of the word "kase." When it finds a match, notice it highlights the word. The prompt "FOUND! Press F7 to search again, or Esc to cancel." appears at the bottom of the screen.

⑤ To repeat the search, press the F7 (Search) function key again.

⑥ Continue to press the F7 (Search) function key until you find the last occurrence of the word. When Q&A Write is finished searching it displays the message "Manual search COMPLETED after 7 matches" at the bottom of the screen.

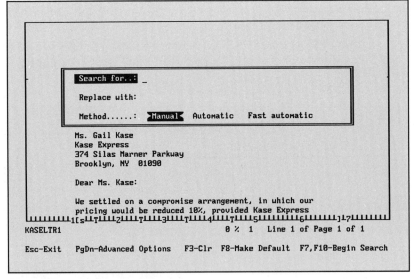

Figure 20.1: The Search dialog box

Replacing Text: Changing a Word

FEATURING

The F7 (Search/Replace) function key

YOU CAN FIND A WORD OR PHRASE AND REPLACE IT with a different word or phrase throughout your document. You can use one of three ways to replace text. You can confirm each change as you move through the document with the Manual option, or you can have Q&A Write replace all occurrences of the word or phrase automatically with the Automatic option. The third method is to find and replace all occurrences without confirmation and without showing the change on the screen. This is called the Fast Auto option.

How to Replace Text

After you find the name Kase throughout the document, you can use the Replace command to change the name to Klaus. Let's try it.

1. Press Ctrl-Home to move the cursor to the top of the document.

2. Press the F7 (Search) function key. The Search dialog box appears.

③ Because you already entered the word "kase" in the "Search for" field, you don't have to enter the text again. Q&A Write remembers the text you last searched for.

④ Press the Enter key to move the cursor to the "Replace with" field, shown in Figure 21.1.

⑤ Type **Klaus** to enter the text you want Q&A Write to use to replace the search text. It does not matter whether you use uppercase or lowercase.

⑥ Press the Enter key to move the cursor to the "Search Method" field.

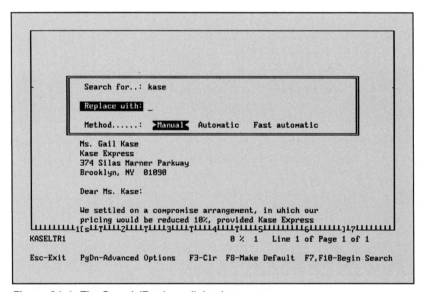

```
        Search for..: kase

       ▌Replace with:▐ _

        Method......: ►Manual◄  Automatic   Fast automatic

        Ms. Gail Kase
        Kase Express
        374 Silas Marner Parkway
        Brooklyn, NY  01090

        Dear Ms. Kase:

        We settled on a compromise arrangement, in which our
        pricing would be reduced 10%, provided Kase Express
└┴┴┴┴┴┴┴┴┴┴1[s┴┴т┴┴┴2┴┴┴т┴┴┴3┴┴┴т┴┴┴4┴┴┴т┴┴┴5┴┴┴┴┴┴┴┴┴6┴┴┴┴┴┴7┴┴┴┴┴┴┴┴
KASELTR1                          0 %  1   Line 1 of Page 1 of 1

Esc-Exit   PgDn-Advanced Options   F3-Clr  F8-Make Default   F7,F10-Begin Search
```

Figure 21.1: The Search/Replace dialog box

⑦ Press the Right-Arrow key to select the "Automatic" search method. The Automatic search method replaces each occurrence without asking you to confirm it and shows each replacement as it happens. Note that Q&A Write replaces text with lightning speed.

(8) Press the F7 (Search) function key to begin searching. Q&A Write searches for the first occurrence of the word. When it finds a match, it replaces the word. When Q&A Write finishes all of the replacements, it displays the message "Automatic search and replace COMPLETED after 7 replacements." at the bottom of the screen.

If you want to take a break now, press Shift-F8 to save your document. Press Enter to accept the file name KASELTR1. Then press ESC to exit the Type/Edit Screen, and press ESC again to exit Q&A Write. You are returned to the Q&A Main Menu.

LESSON 22

Correcting Misspelled Words with the Spelling Checker

FEATURING

The Shift-F1 (Spelling) function key

Q&A WRITE PROVIDES A SPELLING CHECKER FEATURE that contains 100,000 words in its main dictionary. You can use the Spelling Checker to find spelling errors as well as instances where you have accidentally typed the same word twice, and you can easily correct them as you move through the document.

In addition to the main dictionary that Q&A Write provides, you can create your own personal dictionary. You can build the personal dictionary with special technical words that you may use frequently, which are not found in the main dictionary. For example, if you work with legal or medical documents, you can add legal and medical words to the personal dictionary. Q&A Write automatically looks for and loads the main dictionary as well as the personal dictionary when you access the Spelling Checker.

Q&A Write lets you spell check words in two ways. You can either check the spelling of just one word, or check all the words in the document. The Spelling Checker matches the words in the documents with the words in the dictionary. When it finds a word that does not match a word in the dictionary, the Spelling dialog box displays. The Spelling dialog box contains a Spelling menu that lists five options.

You can choose any of the Spelling options to correct each misspelled word. The Spelling menu options are summarized in the list that follows.

List possible spellings	Displays a maximum of nine proposed corrections. You type the number of the word in the list that you want to replace the unmatched word with and press Enter.
Ignore word & continue	Skips over the misspelled word and leaves the word unchanged.
Add to dictionary & continue	Adds the current word to the personal dictionary and continues spell checking.
Add to dictionary & stop	Adds the current word to the personal dictionary and cancels spell checking.
Edit word & recheck	Lets you type the correct word for the misspelled word and then check the corrected word.

You can exit the Spelling Checker any time simply by pressing the Esc (Escape) key. This cancels the spell check operation and returns you to the Type/Edit screen so that you can continue working on your document.

You should run the Spelling Checker as a final proofreading check, before you print a final copy of your document. Spell checking does not totally eliminate the need to proofread for spelling and grammar errors, but it certainly helps.

Since you have made changes to your document with the editing commands, there might not be any misspelled words in your letter. So, before you spell check the document, let's change some of the words and make some intentional spelling errors. Each step sets up a situation, then helps you discover another feature of the Spelling Checker.

How to Spell Check an Entire Document

If you exited Q&A Write in the previous Lesson, Read Lesson 12 on Retrieving Saved Documents to retrieve your letter before starting this lesson.

Let's misspell the word chief and use the overwrite mode to change that word.

① First, position the cursor on the "i" in the word "chief" on line 22.

② Type **ei**.

③ Position the cursor on the "o" in the word "favorable" on line 23.

④ Type **e**.

⑤ Position the cursor on the first "t" in the word "settled" on line 27 in the third paragraph.

⑥ Press the Del (Delete) key.

⑦ Now it is time to begin spell checking the document. Press Ctrl-Home to move the cursor to the top of the document.

⑧ Press Shift-F1 to begin checking for spelling errors. When Q&A Write finds a misspelled word, it highlights the word in the document. The word "Klaus" is highlighted. The prompt "Repeated word. Press F3 to delete, ← to Continue." appears at the bottom of the screen.

⑨ Because Klaus appears in the inside address two times in a row, the Spelling Checker detected this. Press Enter to continue and leave it unchanged.

⑩ The Spelling Checker stops at the name "Marner." The Spelling dialog box appears, as shown in Figure 22.1. You can choose any of the Spelling options to correct each misspelled word.

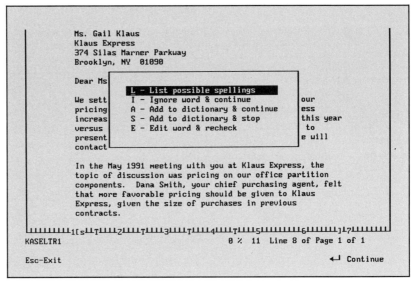

Figure 22.1: *The Spelling dialog box*

⑪ Since "Marner" is a name that is spelled correctly, you can ignore this word and leave it unchanged by selecting the "Ignore word" option. Q&A Write continues spell checking.

⑫ The Spelling Checker stops at the word "cheif" and displays the Spelling dialog box. Press Enter to choose List possible spellings. Q&A Write displays a list of proposed corrections. (This way, you can guess at a correction for a misspelled word.) Press Enter to select the word "chief." Q&A Write replaces the misspelled word with the word you selected from the list and continues spell checking.

⑬ The Spelling Checker stops at the word "faverable" and displays the Spelling dialog box. In this case, choose List possible spellings. Press Enter to select the word "favor-able." Q&A Write replaces the misspelled word with the word you selected from the list and continues spell checking.

⑭ The Spelling Checker stops at the word "setled." Instead of choosing the correct word from the list of possible spellings, choose Edit word & recheck to manually correct the misspelled word.

⑮ Move the cursor to the "t." Press Insert. Then type **t**.

⑯ Press Enter. The word is rechecked and Q&A Write continues spell checking.

⑰ The Spelling Checker stops at your name. Choose the Add to dictionary and continue option. This adds the word to the personal dictionary and continues spell checking. When you have finished spell checking your entire letter, the message "Spelling check COMPLETED" appears at the bottom of the screen. Keep in mind that you can exit the spelling checker any time by pressing Esc.

Using the Thesaurus

FEATURING

The Alt-F1 (Thesaurus) function key

Q&A WRITE ALSO PROVIDES A BUILT-IN THESAURUS containing root words and synonyms. You can use the Thesaurus to look up a synonym or to find out if a word is a verb, noun, adjective, and so forth.

*H*ow to Look Up a Synonym for a Word

Let's look up better words for "arrangement" and "proposal" in your letter.

① Position the cursor on the word "arrangement" on line 13.

② Press the Alt-F1 (Thesaurus) key. The Thesaurus screen appears, as shown in Figure 23.1. The word at the cursor position "arrangement" is highlighted or in a different color in the document, and you are presented with a list of potentially appropriate replacement words.

③ Press the Right-Arrow key to move the cursor through the list of synonyms to find the word "plan."

④ Press F10 to select the synonym. Q&A Write automatically replaces the current word with the synonym you selected.

⑤ Position the cursor on the word "proposal" in the first paragraph.

⑥ Press the Alt-F1 (Thesaurus) key. The Thesaurus screen appears. The word "proposal" at the cursor position is highlighted or in a different color, and you are presented with a list of potentially appropriate replacement words.

⑦ Press the Down-Arrow and Right-Arrow keys to move the cursor through the list of synonyms to find the word "offer."

⑧ Press F10 to select the synonym. Q&A Write automatically replaces the current word with the synonym you selected.

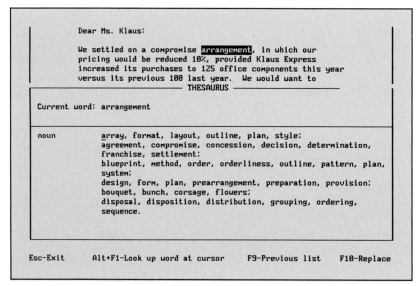

Figure 23.1: The Thesaurus screen

Applying Bold and Underline to Enhance Text

FEATURING

*The Shift-F6 (Enhancements)
function key
Bold and Underline enhancements*

NOW THAT YOU KNOW HOW TO MAKE CHANGES TO YOUR document, check for misspelled words and how to correct them, you're ready to add the finishing touches to your documents. In this section, you will explore how to enhance text in your documents.

Q&A Write gives you several ways to enhance text. You can apply **bold**, <u>underline</u>, ^{super}script, _{sub}script, *italics* and ~~strikeout~~ to change the appearance of individual letters, numbers, and symbols. By applying an enhancement to characters you can make them stand out from surrounding text.

When you apply enhancements to text, on the screen they do not appear exactly as they should. If you have a monochrome or black and white monitor, the enhancements appear highlighted on the screen. If you have a color monitor, the enhancements appear in a different color.

Enhanced text does not always print as it is displayed on the screen. Your printer capabilities determine how the enhanced text prints. To determine exactly which enhancements your printer supports, you can run a printer test and print a list of all the enhancements your printer is capable of printing. Refer to your printer manual for instructions on running the printer test.

In this lesson, you will learn about two of the text enhancements, bold and underline. "Klaus Express" in the heading of your letter can be emphasized with bold to darken and draw attention to it. You can underline "reduced 10%" in the body of the letter to emphasize it.

How to Add Bold and Underline to Enhance Text

Let's try it now and see how it looks.

① Position the cursor on line 7, position 1.

② Press Shift-F6. The Text Enhancements and Fonts menu appears, shown in Figure 24.1.

③ The Bold enhancement is the first item in the menu so you can press Enter. The prompt, "Use the arrow keys to select the text you want to embolden, then press F10" appears at the bottom of the screen.

④ Using the arrow keys, highlight "Klaus Express."

⑤ Press F10. The text is highlighted or in a different color. Notice the "Bold" indicator appears on the Status line next to the document name at the bottom of the screen when the cursor is on the enhanced text.

⑥ Position the cursor on line 14, position 10.

⑦ Press Shift-F6.

⑧ Press U to move the highlight to the Underline enhancement and then press Enter.

⑨ Using the arrow keys, highlight "reduced 10%."

⑩ Press F10. Notice the text appears highlighted or in a different color and does not display the underline. However, you will be able to view the underline with the Page Preview feature when you print your document later in this chapter. Notice the "Undl" indicator appears on the Status line next to the document name at the bottom of the screen when the cursor is on the enhanced text.

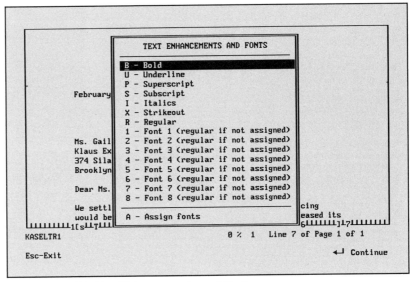

Figure 24.1: *The Text Enhancements and Fonts menu*

Setting Tabs and Margins

AT THE BOTTOM OF THE SCREEN THERE IS A RULER LINE that displays tab stops and margins. Q&A Write's Ruler line is a graphic on-screen helper for setting tab stops. The Ruler line is used to set tab stops but not margins. You enter the margin settings in the Define Page screen.

You can use tabs to position text at a specific place from the left margin. Tab stops are typically used to indent the first line of a paragraph or to create columns in tables or charts. Initially, the tab stops are set in increments of five characters' positions across the Ruler line. A tab stop is represented by a capital T in the Ruler line. You can set and delete tab stops in the document at any time.

Margins are the white space between the text and the edge of a page. You can specify a different set of margins for each document in the Define Page Screen. The left margin is represented by a [(left bracket) symbol on the far left in the Ruler line and the right margin is represented by a] (right bracket) symbol on the far right in the Ruler line. Initially, the margins are set for an 8½ by 11 inch page. The initial margin settings are 10 for the left margin and 68 for the right margin.

The amount of space available for text on a page is affected by the size of the page and the horizontal and vertical orientation of the paper.

When you change margins, if affects every page in your document. Margins may be changed at any time and anywhere in the document.

How to Set Tabs

Let's remove all of the tabs in the Ruler line and set tab stops at 5 and 10.

① Press Ctrl-Home to position the cursor at the top of the document.

② Press F8 to access the Options menu.

③ Press the Right-Arrow key to move the highlight to the submenu.

④ Press the Down-Arrow key to move the highlight to "Set tabs" in the submenu, shown in Figure 25.1.

⑤ Press Enter. The Options menu disappears and the cursor moves to the Ruler line, shown in Figure 25.2. A Tab menu appears at the bottom of the screen that shows commands for working with tabs in the Ruler line. Pressing the Tab key moves the cursor to the next tab in the Ruler line, pressing Shift-Tab moves the cursor to the previous tab in the Ruler line, and pressing F10 saves the changes you make to the Ruler line and returns you to your document.

⑥ Let's see how you move the cursor in the Ruler line. To move to the right, hold down the Right-Arrow key until the cursor cannot move any further, at position 57. The Position indicator at the bottom of the screen on the right should display 57.

⑦ Hold down the Left-Arrow key to move the cursor left on the Ruler line until the cursor is at position 3. Position 3 is always the starting position when you enter the Ruler line. The Position indicator at the bottom of the screen on the right should display 3.

LESSON 25

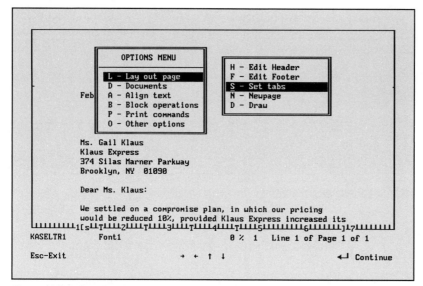

Figure 25.1: *The Set Tabs option in the Options menu*

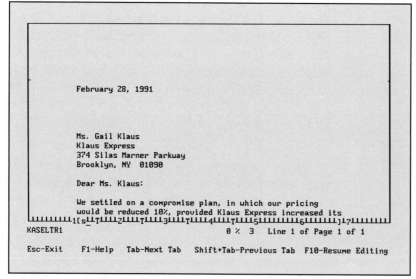

Figure 25.2: *The Ruler Line and Tab menu*

⑧ Move the cursor to the first T or tab stop in the Ruler line. Press the Spacebar to remove the tab stop. The T disappears.

⑨ Move the cursor to each tab stop in the Ruler line and press the Spacebar until you have removed all the tab stops.

⑩ Move the cursor to position 5 and type **t**. A capital T appears in the Ruler line at position 5.

⑪ Move the cursor to position 10 and type **t**. Another capital T appears in the Ruler line.

⑫ Press F10 to exit the Ruler line and return to your document in the Type/Edit screen.

*H*ow to Set Margins

You will change the right margin to 75 and then change it back to 68.

① Let's take a look at where the right margin is set in the Ruler line. Press the Right-Arrow key to move the cursor to position 68. Notice the block cursor in the Ruler line is at position 68 where the] (right bracket) is displayed; however, the position number in the Status line is displayed as 58. The difference between these numbers is 10 characters: Position 1 is set 10 characters from the left edge of the screen, therefore, when you add 10 to 58, you get a right margin of 68.

② Press Ctrl-F6 to access the Define Page screen, as shown in Figure 25.3.

③ Press Enter to move the highlight to the "Right margin" setting.

④ Type **75**.

⑤ Press F10 to accept the new right margin setting and exit the Define Page screen. You are returned to your document. Notice the text in your document automatically adjusts to the new right margin and the] (right bracket) in the Ruler line is at position 75.

(6) Press Ctrl-F6 to bring up the Define Page screen again. Let's change the right margin back to 68.

(7) Press Enter to move the highlight to the "Right margin" setting.

(8) Type **68**.

(9) Press F10 to accept the new right margin setting and exit the Define Page screen. You are returned to your document. Notice the text in your document automatically adjusts to the new right margin and the] (right bracket) in the Ruler line is at position 68.

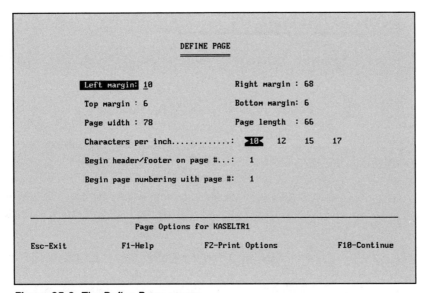

Figure 25.3: *The Define Page screen*

Aligning Text

FEATURING
The Tab key
Centering text

YOU CAN USE A TAB TO INDENT THE FIRST LINE OF a paragraph from the left margin. The text wraps to the left margin.

You can use multiple tab stops to indent a paragraph as much as you want. For example, if tab stops are set in increments of five, press the Tab key once. The text indents at 5. If you press the Tab key twice, the text indents at 10.

*H*ow to Indent Text

For practice, let's indent the first and second paragraph with a tab.

① Position the cursor at the beginning of the first paragraph.

② Press the Ins (Insert) key.

③ Press the Tab key, usually located to the left of the letter "Q" on your keyboard. Notice the first line is indented at position 5 and the rest of the lines in the paragraph wrap to the left margin.

④ Position the cursor at the beginning of the second paragraph.

LESSON 26

⑤ Press the Tab key. Notice the first line is indented at position 5 and the rest of the lines in the paragraph wrap to the left margin.

⑥ Position the cursor at the beginning of the second paragraph.

⑦ Press the Tab key. Notice the first line is indented at position 5 and the rest of the lines in the paragraph wrap to the left margin, as shown in Figure 26.1.

⑧ Press the Ins (Insert) key to exit Insert mode.

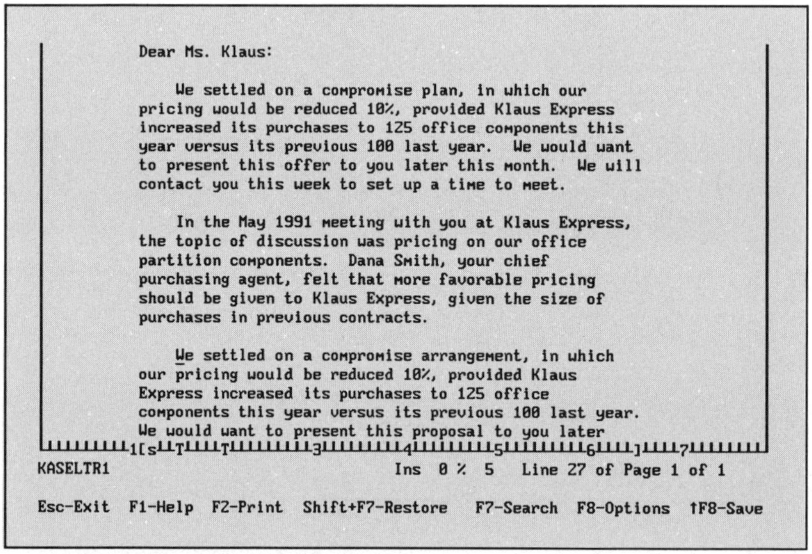

```
Dear Ms. Klaus:

      We settled on a compromise plan, in which our
pricing would be reduced 10%, provided Klaus Express
increased its purchases to 125 office components this
year versus its previous 100 last year.  We would want
to present this offer to you later this month.  We will
contact you this week to set up a time to meet.

      In the May 1991 meeting with you at Klaus Express,
the topic of discussion was pricing on our office
partition components.  Dana Smith, your chief
purchasing agent, felt that more favorable pricing
should be given to Klaus Express, given the size of
purchases in previous contracts.

      We settled on a compromise arrangement, in which
our pricing would be reduced 10%, provided Klaus
Express increased its purchases to 125 office
components this year versus its previous 100 last year.
We would want to present this proposal to you later

KASELTR1                        Ins  0 %  5   Line 27 of Page 1 of 1

Esc-Exit  F1-Help  F2-Print  Shift+F7-Restore   F7-Search  F8-Options  ↑F8-Save
```

Figure 26.1: Indented paragraphs with a tab

You can center text between the left and right margins. This is useful especially when you want to center a short line such as a title.

How to Center Text

In this lesson, you will practice how to center text by first typing a line of text at the bottom of your letter and then centering it.

① Press Ctrl-End to move the cursor to the bottom of the document.

② Position the cursor on line 43.

③ Type **This is a centered line.** Then press Enter.

④ Press the Up-Arrow key to move the cursor back to line 43.

⑤ Press F8 to access the Options menu.

⑥ Press A to move the highlight to "Align text."

⑦ Press the Right-Arrow key to move the highlight to the submenu.

⑧ Press C to move the highlight to the "Center" option.

⑨ Press Enter. Notice the line is now centered, as shown in Figure 26.2.

If you want to take a break now, press Shift-F8 to save your document. Press Enter to accept the file name KASELTER1. Then press Esc to exit the Type / Edit screen, and press Esc again to exit Q&A Write. You are returned to the Q&A Main Menu.

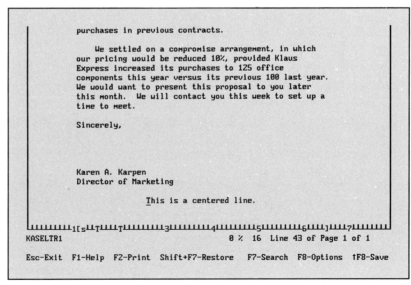

Figure 26.2: *A centered line*

Inserting Page Breaks

FEATURING

The F8 (Options) function key
Newpage command for inserting
page breaks

TO DIVIDE THE TEXT INTO PAGES YOU CAN INSERT PAGE
breaks throughout your document. This process is called pagination.
The page break signal tells the printer when to stop printing one page
and to begin printing the next page.

You can specify a new page at the places where you want a page
break anywhere in the document. Pages are not affected by editing or
formatting changes you make and do not change unless you move or
remove them.

You can force a new page to ensure a page break at a specified
position. For example, you may want to place a title and its text on a
new page. This feature is useful when you want to keep charts and text
together on the same page.

How to Insert a Page Break

If you exited Q&A Write in the previous Lesson, read Lesson 12 on
Retrieving Saved Documents to retrieve your letter before this lesson.

Let's insert a page break to divide your document into two pages.

① Position the cursor on line 43, position 1. This is where you will enter the page break. This line will be the first line on the new page.

② Press F8 to bring up the Options menu.

③ Press the Right-Arrow key to move the highlight to the submenu.

④ Press N to select Newpage and press Enter. You are returned to your document. The cursor is now on page 2. Notice the page number indicator, Page 2 of 2 in the Status line at the bottom of the screen.

⑤ Press the Up-Arrow key to move the cursor to page 1. The page break code appears in your document, as shown in Figure 27.1.

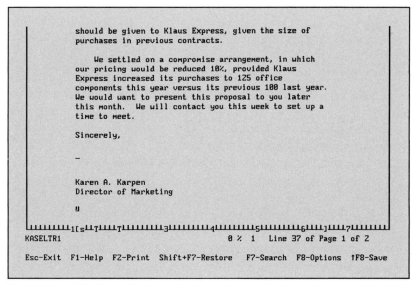

Figure 27.1: *The Page Break code*

Adding Headers and Footers

FEATURING

The F8 (Options) function key
Edit Header command
Edit Footer command

A HEADER IS TEXT THAT APPEARS AT THE TOP OF EVERY page; usually it is only a few words long. A footer is text that appears at the bottom of every page. Headers and footers often contain page numbers, chapter titles, document titles, dates, or the author's name.

In Q&A Write, you can easily insert a header or footer that is the same on every page. Note that the first page or title page does not usually contain a header or footer.

The header and footer information you enter is printed within the top and bottom margins respectively. The top and bottom margins are initially set for 1 inch, which is equivalent to 6 lines. If your header and footer information takes up 6 lines or more, you must change the top and bottom margins accordingly in the Define Page screen. Otherwise when Q&A Write prints the document, the header and footer information will either completely cover or overlap the text in the document.

How to Add a Header

Let's set up a header that repeats your name at the top of every page. Then you will learn how to number pages automatically.

① From the Type/Edit screen, press F8 to display the Options menu.

② Press the Right-Arrow key to move the highlight to the submenu.

③ Since "Edit Header" is the command we want and it is the first command in the menu, simply press Enter to select it. The Header window appears, as shown in Figure 28.1. Notice the Header command menu at the bottom of the screen.

④ Type your name in the Header window and press Enter.

⑤ Press F10 to exit the Header Window and return to your document.

⑥ To view the header information, press the Down-Arrow key to move to page 2. You will also be able to view the header information in the document when you use the Page Preview feature in Lesson 29.

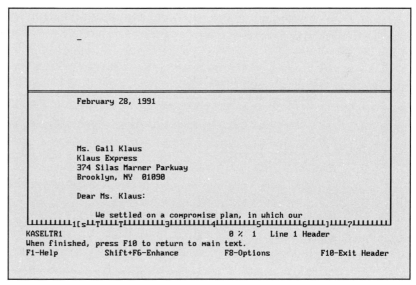

Figure 28.1: *The Header window*

Page numbers typically are a part of a header or footer. To number the pages of a Q&A Write document, insert a page number as part of the header or footer.

How to Add a Footer and Number Pages Automatically

For practice, let's number the pages in your letter by setting up a footer and specifying page numbers for the document.

① From the Type/Edit screen, press F8 to display the Options menu.

② Press the Right-Arrow key to move the highlight to the submenu.

③ Press the Down-Arrow key to move the highlight to "Edit Footer."

④ Press Enter. The Footer window appears.

⑤ Type a # (number symbol) in the Footer window and press Enter.

⑥ To center the # symbol so that your page numbers are centered at the bottom of each page, you can press F8 to access the Options menu.

⑦ Press A to move the highlight to Align text and then press Enter.

⑧ Press the Right-Arrow key to move the submenu.

⑨ Press C to select Center.

⑩ Press Enter. The # symbol should be centered in the Footer window, as shown in Figure 28.2.

⑪ Press F10 to exit the Footer Window and to return to your document.

⑫ The next step is to tell Q&A Write which page you want to start numbering and the number you want to start with.

Let's start numbering on page 2 with the number 2. Press Ctrl-F6 to access the Define Page screen.

⑬ Press Enter seven times to move the highlight to the option "Begin header/footer on page #."

⑭ Type **2** and press Enter.

⑮ The cursor moves to the option "Begin page numbering with Page #". Type **2** and press Enter.

⑯ Press F10 to save the changes you made for page numbering in the Define Page screen. You are returned to your document.

⑰ To view the Footer information, using the Down-Arrow Key, move the cursor to line 54 on page 2. Notice the page number is centered. You will also be able to view the page numbers when you use the Page Preview feature in the next lessons.

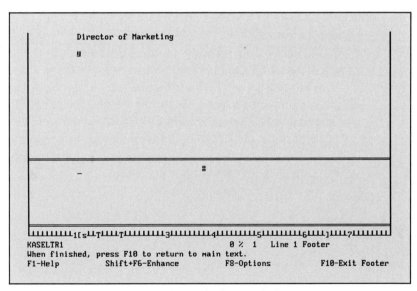

Figure 28.2: *Page number symbol in the footer window*

Using Page Preview

FEATURING

*The F2 (Print Options) function
key
The Page Preview command*

BEFORE YOU PRINT YOUR DOCUMENT, YOU CAN SEE HOW
it will look by previewing it on your screen. You can then make the
necessary changes before printing a final, formatted copy.

You can use the Page Preview feature to see how your document
will look when it is printed. A miniature version of the formatted
pages appears on your screen. You can see the placement and appearance of headers and footers, page numbers, fonts, enhancements, and
margins as well as standard tabs and centered text. However, you cannot edit or format text in Page Preview mode. You must switch back
to the Type/Edit screen to edit your document.

How to Use Page Preview

Let's take a look at the document with Page Preview to see how
the letter will look when it is printed.

① Press F2 to bring up the Print Options screen.

② Press Enter seven times to move the highlight to the "Page
Preview" option on the Print Options screen.

③ Press the Spacebar to set Page Preview to Yes.

④ Press F10. You are presented with the Page Preview screen that displays your document in Full Page mode, as shown in Figure 29.1. Notice the Page Preview menu at the bottom of the screen.

⑤ Press + (plus) to select Zoom in and expand the page. Notice "Klaus Express" in the inside address appears in bold text. "Reduced 10%" in the first sentence is underlined.

⑥ Press – (minus) to select Zoom out and shrink the page.

⑦ Press Ctrl-PgDn to see the header and footer information on page 2 of your document.

⑧ Press Ctrl-PgUp to see the first page of your document.

⑨ Press Esc to exit Page Preview mode.

⑩ Let's set Page Preview back to No in the Print Options screen. Press F2 to access the Print Options screen.

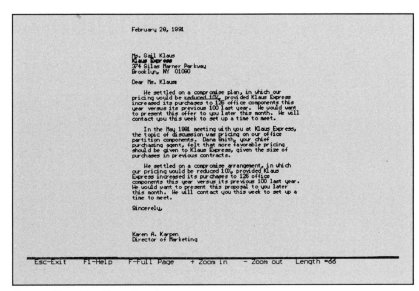

Figure 29.1: *The Page Preview screen*

⑪ Press Enter seven times to move the highlight to the "Page Preview" option on the Print Options screen.

⑫ Press the Spacebar to set Page Preview back to No.

⑬ Press F-9 to save the change and exit the Print Options screen.

Printing a Document

FEATURING

The F2 (Print Options) function key

AFTER YOU PREVIEW YOUR DOCUMENT ON THE SCREEN, you can make the necessary changes. Then you are ready to print a final copy of your document. A final copy of a document includes the correct font and type size and enhancements such as bold and underline.

Before you print, you can change any of the print options on the Print Options screen. You can specify the number of pages you want to print with the From page and To page options. You can indicate the number of copies you want to print with the Number of Copies option.

The Line Spacing option allows you to specify double spacing so you can print a draft copy of your document. The initial setting is single spacing. The Type of Paper Feed option lets you specify printing on single sheets of paper or continuous form pin-feed paper. Initially, it is set to Continuous.

How to Print a Document

Let's print the letter and then save the document.

① Press F2 to access the Print Options screen. The Print Options screen appears, shown in Figure 30.1.

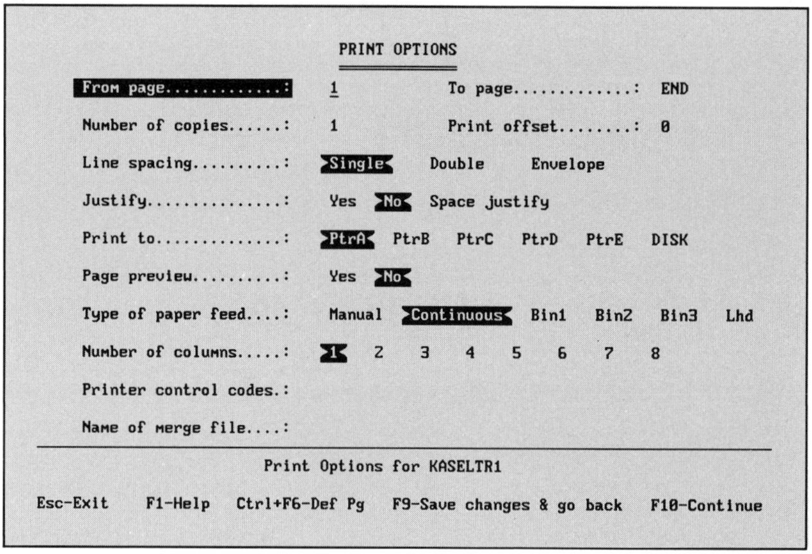

```
                            PRINT OPTIONS

     From page............:   1              To page............:  END

     Number of copies......:  1              Print offset........:  0

     Line spacing..........:  >Single<   Double     Envelope

     Justify...............:  Yes  >No<  Space justify

     Print to..............:  >PtrA<  PtrB   PtrC   PtrD   PtrE   DISK

     Page preview..........:  Yes  >No<

     Type of paper feed....:  Manual  >Continuous<  Bin1   Bin2   Bin3   Lhd

     Number of columns.....:  >1<   2    3    4    5    6    7    8

     Printer control codes.:

     Name of merge file....:
     _____
                      Print Options for KASELTR1

  Esc-Exit    F1-Help    Ctrl+F6-Def Pg    F9-Save changes & go back    F10-Continue
```

Figure 30.1: *The Print Options screen*

② Read the screen to learn about the print options available. Let's not change any of them. This way, we can print the document using the initial settings very easily.

③ Simply press F10 to continue. A Print dialog box appears and tells you how many pages are printing. After the document finishes printing, take a look at your printed letter. You now have the first masterpiece that you created using Q&A Write.

④ To save the document, press Shift-F8.

⑤ Press Enter to accept the file name KASELTR1. Now the print settings are stored with your document.

LESSON **31**

Backing Up the Document to a Floppy Disk

FEATURING

The Utilities option
The DOS facilities option
The Copy a document option

TO ENSURE THE SAFETY OF THE DOCUMENTS YOU CREATE in Q&A Write, it is very important to back up your documents to a floppy disk. You can back up the documents with the Copy a document option in the Q&A Write Utilities and DOS facilities menus. It is a simple procedure that doesn't take long to do and can save you a lot of time and work in the long run.

By copying your documents from the hard disk to floppy disks you will have a second copy of your document just in case there is a system problem or a power failure. If you lost the original documents on the hard disk, you would have to create new documents and retype all of the information.

How to Copy a Document to a Floppy Disk

Let's copy the KASELTR1 document to a floppy disk. Remember, a copy of the document will be on the floppy disk as well as a copy of it remaining on the hard disk, thereby leaving you with two copies of the same document.

LESSON 31

①   Insert a formatted floppy disk in Drive A.

②   Press Esc to exit the Type/Edit screen and return to the Q&A Write menu.

③   Press U to move the highlight to the Utilities option.

④   Press Enter.

⑤   Press D to move the highlight to the DOS facilities option.

⑥   Press Enter.

⑦   Press C to move the highlight to Copy a document and press Enter. The "Copy from" prompt appears in a dialog box.

⑧   Type **kaseltr1** and press Enter. This tells Q&A Write which document you want to copy. The "Copy to" prompt appears.

⑨   Type **a:\kaseltr1**. Compare the dialog box on your screen to the dialog box in Figure 31.1.

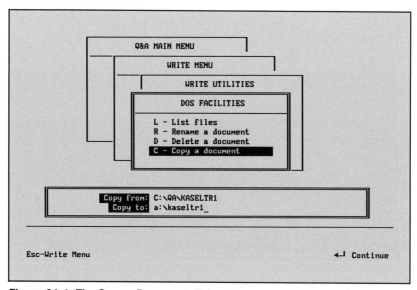

Figure 31.1: The Copy a Document dialog box

⑩ Press Enter. Q&A Write copies the document from the hard disk to the floppy disk. When it is finished with the copy procedure, the prompt "Copy operation COMPLETED" appears at the bottom of the screen. Now you have a copy of your document on the floppy disk. The original document remains on the hard disk.

⑪ Press Esc twice to exit the Q&A Utilities menu and return to the Q&A Write menu.

⑫ Remove the diskette from the Drive A.

Exiting Q&A Write

FEATURING

The Exit option

WHEN YOU ARE FINISHED WORKING IN THE Q&A WRITE
program and you have saved all of your work, you can exit Q&A
Write.

How to Exit Q&A Write

Press Esc to exit the Q&A Write menu. You are returned to the
Q&A Main Menu.

PART

THREE

Q&A File

Starting Q&A File

FEATURING

The Q&A File menu options

WITH Q&A FILE YOU CAN CREATE A DATABASE TO store and retrieve the information you deal with every day. Q&A File works with all kinds of information about people, places, ideas, objects, or events. The database organizes and stores information efficiently, providing easy access to any information you want.

To load the Q&A File program into your computer's memory, simply select File from the Q&A Main Menu and press Enter. Then you are ready to create a new database file.

The Q&A File menu displays nine menu options. These options are summarized in the following list:

Design file	Creates, edits and customizes forms in a database file.
Add data	Enters data into forms.
Search/Update	Finds specific records, changes information in the records.
Print	Prints some or all of the records.
Copy	Copies the database file design, data, or both to disk.
Remove	Deletes a group of records or duplicate records.

Mass Update	Changes information on a group of records.
Post	Posts data to multiple fields in external database files.
Utilities	Imports and exports data, backs up a database to disk, recovers damaged Q&A File database files.

The first menu option, Design file, appears highlighted or in a different color on the screen. The Design file option is used for several purposes: for example, creating, editing, and customizing the design of your database. To select an option from the Q&A File menu, you can use the arrow keys and then press Enter, or you can press the letter corresponding to the menu option and then press Enter. For the purposes of the lessons that follow, you will be using the second method to select options from Q&A File menus.

At the bottom of the menu is the key assignment line. If you press Esc you will return to the Q&A Main Menu. If you press the F1 (Help) key to select the Description of Choices option on the key assignment line at the bottom of the screen, you will see a Help screen that further explains the options in the Q&A File menu. If you press the Enter key you will continue to the next screen.

If you follow the steps in the lessons in Part Three, you will be working with a typical database and accumulate some hands-on experience with Q&A File. Once you complete the lessons, you should have a good understanding of how to create a simple database using Q&A File and you will be ready to start designing databases of your own.

*H*ow to Start Q&A File

Let's begin now.

① To start Q&A File, notice that the File option in the Q&A Main Menu is the first option and that it is already highlighted.

② Press the Enter key. The Q&A File menu appears on the screen, as shown in Figure 33.1.

LESSON 33

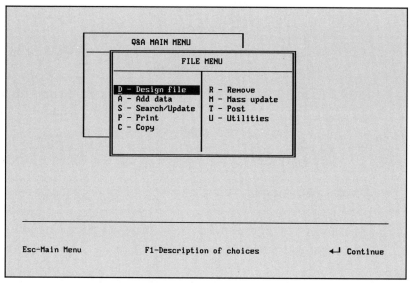

Figure 33.1: *The Q&A File menu*

Creating a Database File

FEATURING

The Design file option,
Database terms and concepts

THE TERM DATABASE IS COMPUTER JARGON FOR A familiar and essential item in our everyday lives. A database is a collection of information organized to serve a specific purpose. The telephone directory is one familiar database example. This database contains the names, addresses, and telephone numbers of individuals, businesses, and government agencies. Other common database examples are personnel files, client lists, membership lists, and inventories.

Q&A File operates on the principle that information is kept in forms, just as businesses keep records on paper. When you use Q&A File, you design the form yourself, modelling its structure from familiar paper forms, or creating a new design precisely suited to your needs. You type the design and then you save it in a file on the hard disk. Later, you use the form design to store your information and retrieve it when you want to review, update, or print selected forms.

To become comfortable with the way Q&A works, you should become acquainted with the following four important terms used to discuss databases.

① A **field** contains the variable items of information that make up each record. If only names, addresses, and phone numbers are included in the telephone directory database, each record contains three fields, name, address, and phone number.

② **A record** is a unit of information within a file. Within the telephone directory database each business associate's name, address, and phone number represents one record. If you include 25 business associates' names, addresses and phone numbers you will have 25 records within that file.

③ **A form** is the visual representation of the structure of the database record. It shows the appearance of the record by displaying various sizes, shapes, and content. A form is used to display data, retrieve data, and prepare reports.

④ **A database** is a collection of records stored in a single file on disk. The records contain related information. As each database is created it is given a file name. For example, a database containing the names, addresses, and phone numbers of all your business associates can be created and stored with the name PHONE.

There are several technical specifications and maximum limits established by Symantec for the Q&A File program. You should become acquainted with these when you are setting up your database files. The following list summarizes these specifications and maximum limits:

Pages per form	10
Fields per record	2,045
Fields per page	248
Characters per record	65,536
Characters per field	32,768
Records per database	534,288
File size	1,024 megabytes (million characters)

To create a database file in Q&A File, you must first design the layout of the database. Q&A File provides a blank form on the screen where you will be designing your database. The form can have up to ten screen pages. Each screen page contains 21 lines. Three screen pages fit on a standard 8½ by 11 printed page of 66 lines.

At the bottom of the blank form on the screen there is a Status line, a message line, a key assignment line, and a Ruler line.

The Status line shows the name of the database and the amount of memory used. For example, 0% means the database form is empty or has very few characters in it. The Status line also displays the current position of the cursor on the screen. The key assignment line displays Q&A File's design database form functions with their corresponding function keys. The Ruler line displays tab stops.

How to Create a Database File

Now that you are familiar with some basic database concepts and terms, it is time to design your first database called EMPLOYEE.

① To begin creating a database file, the Design file option in the Q&A File menu should be highlighted. If it isn't, then press D to highlight Design file now.

② Press the Enter key. The Design menu appears, as shown in Figure 34.1.

③ The Design a new file option is already highlighted. Press Enter to select it.

④ Q&A File prompts you to enter the name of the new file. The file name can have one to eight characters, letters, numbers, or both, and cannot have spaces or punctuation.

⑤ Type **employee** and press Enter. Q&A File automatically assigns the file extension .DTF to the file name. DTF stands for data file and is used to distinguish database files from other files in Q&A. The complete file name is EMPLOYEE.DTF.

⑥ A blank form appears on the screen, as shown in Figure 34.2, ready for you to design the layout of your database. Notice the cursor is in the upper-left corner of the

LESSON 34

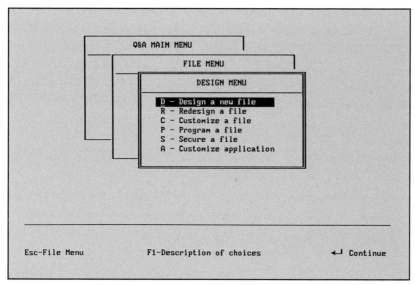

Figure 34.1: *The Design menu*

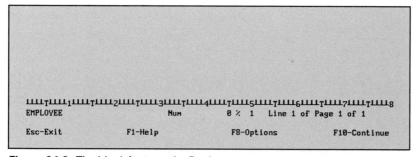

Figure 34.2: *The blank form on the Design screen*

screen. The database file name EMPLOYEE appears at the bottom of the screen on the left. The Num indicator tells you that the numeric keypad is engaged. The Ruler line at the bottom shows you the tab stops. Each tab stop is represented by a capital letter T. The Status line shows the percentage of memory used, as well as the position of the cursor. Currently, the cursor is on line 1 and page 1 of the form.

Remember, a form can have a maximum of 10 pages. The key assignment line gives you four options. You can press Esc to exit the form. Press the F1 (Help) function key to get help on designing a form; press the F8 (Options) function key to access the special features for designing a form; and press the F10 key to continue to the next screen.

Entering the Database Field Labels

FEATURING

Design layout
The database form and field labels

IN THE DATABASE FORM, YOU CREATE A PLACE TO STORE your information. *The structure and layout of the database must be created before the actual data is input.* You can create an image of the form you want.

When you create forms of your own, you can copy familiar paper forms you have on hand, or you can use the following guidelines to design a new form.

Before entering database field labels, identify the format and information that you will need. Determine what kind of reports will be generated from the database and what kind of information is necessary. Try to identify all the uses for the database to ensure that all the necessary information will be included in each record.

There are four questions to ask yourself before you start to enter field labels in the blank form:

- What fields do I want to have?

- What shall I name the fields?

- What types of information will these fields contain?

- How much space should I leave for each item of information?

A field label is entered into the blank form to identify the kind of information that will be typed into the field. Each field must have a unique name or label. You must not enter any duplicate labels. If you do enter duplicates, you won't be able to search a particular field to find the specific information you want.

To enter a field label, use the arrow keys to move the cursor to the place where you want the name to appear. Then type the name onto the blank form on the screen. *Each field label must end with a colon.* For instance, Last name: indicates that only the last name should be entered in that particular field. More than one field label can be entered on the same line.

When typing, don't worry about making errors. If you do catch an error while typing, use the Backspace key (usually located in the upper-right corner of your keyboard) to erase it.

To determine how much space to leave between field labels, you need to know where a field ends. A field can end at the right side of the screen, the end or bottom of the screen, at the start of another field, or where it encounters a line character such as a field within a box. You will draw lines and boxes on your form later to make it look like a typical paper form.

Note: If a field takes up more than one line, you must indicate the end of the field by typing the greater than symbol ($>$) at the end of the field. Otherwise, Q&A File will treat the field as a single line and ignore the rest of the lines in the field.

How to Enter Database Field Labels

You will enter field labels in the blank form to store typical personnel information for a commercial interior design company called Office Designs. Let's enter the field labels in capital letters so that they will look different from the data that you will input later. That way, you differentiate between the field label and the actual data within a field. Do not forget to add a colon at the end of the field label. Do not type the period that follows the instruction.

① To begin entering database field labels, press Enter. This way, you will start typing on line 2. Also you are leaving enough space around the field labels so that later on you can draw lines to enclose the information in a box.

② With the cursor on line 2, press the Spacebar to move the cursor to position 2. Type **LAST NAME:** Notice the block cursor in the Ruler line moves as you enter information to reflect the current position of the cursor. Make sure to enter the colon symbol. It marks the beginning of the field.

③ Press the Tab key three times to move the cursor to position 35. Type **FIRST NAME:** You have now completed the first line of the form by entering two field labels.

④ Press Enter twice. The cursor moves to line 4. Check the Status line to confirm that the cursor is on line 4.

⑤ Press the Spacebar and type **ADDRESS:**. (Do not type the period.) With one space before the field label, this allows enough room to draw lines around the information later.

⑥ Press Enter twice. The cursor moves to line 6.

⑦ Press the Spacebar and type **CITY:**. (Do not type the period.)

⑧ Press the Tab key twice to move the cursor to position 25.

⑨ Type **STATE:**.

⑩ Press the Tab key once to move the cursor to position 35 and type **ZIP:**.

⑪ Press Enter twice. The cursor moves to line 8.

⑫ Press the Spacebar and type **EMP ID#:**.

⑬ Press the Tab key twice to move the cursor to position 25 and type **HOME PHONE:**.

⑭ Press Enter twice. The cursor moves to line 10.

⑮ Press the Spacebar, then type **HIRED DT:**.

⑯ Press the Tab key twice to move the cursor to position 25 and type **JOB TITLE:**.

⑰ Press the Tab key twice to move the cursor to position 55 and type **SALARY:**.

⑱ Press the Caps Lock key.

⑲ You have now completed entering the field labels for your database. Compare the form on your screen to the form shown in Figure 35.1.

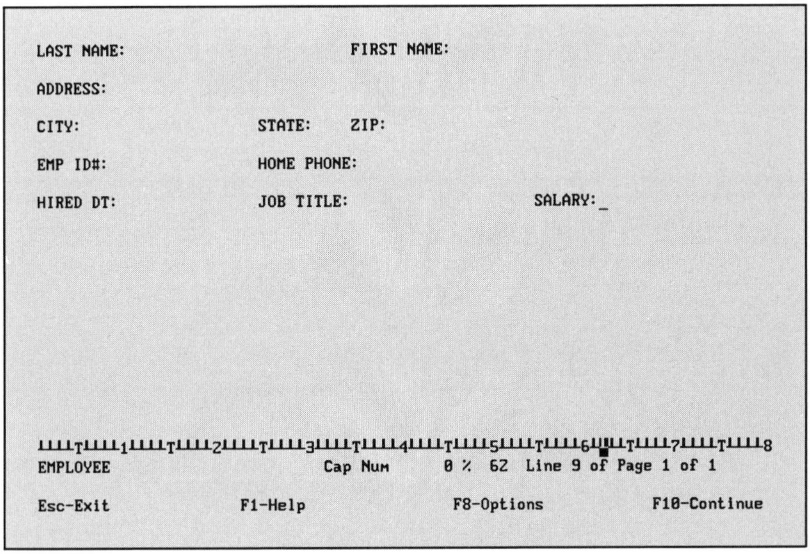

```
LAST NAME:                    FIRST NAME:

ADDRESS:

CITY:            STATE:    ZIP:

EMP ID#:         HOME PHONE:

HIRED DT:        JOB TITLE:              SALARY:_




LLLLTLLLL1LLLLTLLLL2LLLLTLLL3LLLLTLLLL4LLLLTLLLL5LLLLTLLLL6LLLLTLLLL7LLLLTLLLL8
EMPLOYEE                  Cap Num     0 % 62  Line 9 of Page 1 of 1

Esc-Exit         F1-Help              F8-Options          F10-Continue
```

Figure 35.1: *The Design Form with the sample database*

Drawing Lines and Boxes

FEATURING

The Options menu
Lay out page option
Draw option

ONE OF THE REALLY NICE THINGS ABOUT Q&A FILE IS that you can make your form on the screen look like the paper form you use in your office; that is, you can draw lines and boxes on your form. That way, you can visually divide one area of a form from another or focus attention on specific parts of the form.

Note that lines do not always print as they are displayed on your screen. The capabilities of your printer determine how the lines print. Your printer must have the IBM box graphics characters in order to print lines and boxes. To determine if your printer supports IBM box graphics characters, refer to your printer manual and to the Q&A documentation. If your printer does not have the capability to print these characters, Q&A substitutes dashes, pluses, and other symbols on your printout.

How to Draw Lines and Boxes

Let's use the Draw feature to draw some lines and boxes now. We will separate the name and address information from the phone and job information and enclose each section in a box.

①　To move the cursor to the top of the form, press Ctrl-Home. The cursor is positioned on line 1.

②　Press F8 to access the Options menu, shown in Figure 36.1.

③　Because the Lay out page option is the first option on the menu and is already highlighted, press the Right-Arrow key to move the highlight to the submenu.

④　The Set tabs option is highlighted. Press D to move the highlight to the Draw option.

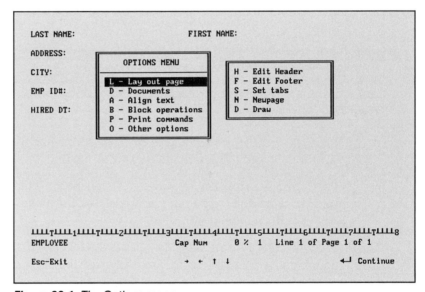

Figure 36.1: *The Options menu*

⑤　Press Enter. The prompt at the bottom of the screen asks you to use the arrow keys to draw horizontal and vertical lines. The Draw menu appears below the prompt, as shown in Figure 36.2. Let's explore using the keys shown in the Draw menu by drawing the lines on the form.

⑥　Hold down the Right-Arrow key and draw a horizontal line until the cursor is at position 75 on line 1.

⑦　Press the Down-Arrow key to draw a vertical line until the cursor is on line 7.

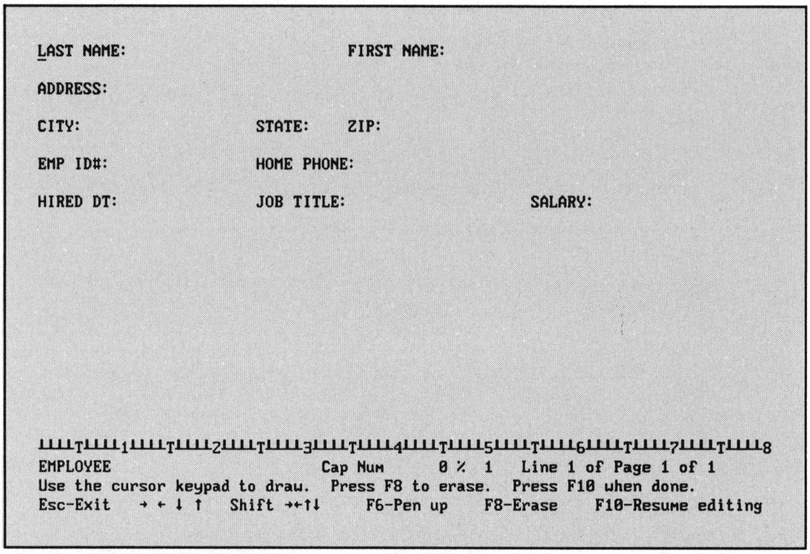

Figure 36.2: *The Draw menu*

(8) Press the Left-Arrow key and draw a horizontal line from right to left until the cursor is at position 1 on line 7.

(9) Press the Up-Arrow key to draw a vertical line until the cursor is back on line 1. You have now enclosed the name and address information inside a box.

(10) Press F6. This lifts the drawing pen off the form so that you do not create a line when you press an arrow key.

(11) Using the Down-Arrow key, move the cursor to line 7.

(12) Press F6 to return to drawing. Draw a vertical line down to line 11. If you make a mistake and you want to erase a line, press F8. Then press the appropriate arrow key to erase the line. Press F8 again to return to drawing.

(13) Draw a horizontal line on line 11 to position 75.

(14) Draw a vertical line up to line 7.

(15) When you are finished with the Draw option, press F10 to save the lines and boxes you created. This returns you to the

form. Compare your form to the sample form shown in Figure 36.3.

16 Press F10 to save the field labels and the layout of the form. The message "Saving Design" flashes in the lower-left corner of the screen. Then Q&A displays the Format Spec where you can assign information types. The Format Spec is discussed in the next lesson.

```
┌──────────────────────────────────────────────────────────────────┐
│ LAST NAME:                         FIRST NAME:                      │
│ ADDRESS:                                                            │
│ CITY:              STATE:    ZIP:                                   │
│ EMP ID#:           HOME PHONE:                                      │
│ HIRED DT:          JOB TITLE:              SALARY:                  │
└──────────────────────────────────────────────────────────────────┘




   ⌊⌊⌊⌊T⌊⌊⌊⌊₁⌊⌊⌊⌊T⌊⌊⌊⌊₂⌊⌊⌊⌊T⌊⌊⌊⌊₃⌊⌊⌊⌊T⌊⌊⌊⌊₄⌊⌊⌊⌊T⌊⌊⌊⌊₅⌊⌊⌊⌊T⌊⌊⌊⌊₆⌊⌊⌊⌊T⌊⌊⌊⌊₇⌊⌊⌊⌊T⌊⌊⌊⌊₈
   EMPLOYEE                   Cap Num Ins  1 %  75  Line 7 of Page 1 of 1

   Esc-Exit          F1-Help              F8-Options          F10-Continue
```

Figure 36.3: *Database Form with lines and boxes*

Defining Information Types

FEATURING

The Format Spec

THE COMPUTER HANDLES DIFFERENT KINDS OF DATA IN different ways. So, the next step is to tell it which kind of data is contained in each field. This is called the *information type.* The information type is assigned to each field in the Format Spec. When you define an information type in the Format Spec, you are restricting the contents of the information you can enter in that field. Q&A File formats the information you enter in a database according to the Format Spec.

Each field can be one of seven types and is represented by a code. The information types and codes are summarized in the following list:

Text	T	Conceptual information such as name, address, phone number
Number	N	Quantities, numbers for calculations
Dates	D	Dates only
Yes/No	Y	Answers to Yes/No, True/False questions.
Money	M	Dollars and cents formatting
Hours	H	Times only
Keyword	K	Special searching, categorizing

When you define the Date, Hours, Number, or Money information types, Q&A asks you to set a Global Formatting option for each information type. A Global Formatting option will reformat all date, time, currency, and decimal entries automatically. That way, you can enter the information any way you want to and Q&A File will automatically change it to the format you set in the Global Format Options screen. For example, the Date format can be set to June 15, 1992 or 15 Jun 1992.

After you enter the field labels and design the layout of the form for your database, you are ready to define the information types. All of the fields in your form are text fields except for the Hired Dt field, which is a Date field.

How to Define Information Types

Let's define the Date information type for that field by entering the letter D next to the field label.

① With the Format Spec on your screen, notice that the field labels are highlighted or appear in a different color. A highlighted bar is pointing to the first field, LAST NAME and a flashing cursor appears under the T next to LAST NAME. Also the letter T appears after each field label, as shown in Figure 37.1. It is the code that represents Text.

② Using the Tab key, move the highlighted bar and the flashing cursor to the field label HIRED DT:.

③ Type **D**. This indicates a Date field. Compare your form to the sample form shown in Figure 37.2

④ Press F10. This saves the information type you defined.

⑤ After defining information types, Q&A displays the Global Format Options screen, shown in Figure 37.3. Using the Tab key, move the cursor to the Date option. Q&A gives you 20 different date formats to choose from.

⑥ Using the Right-Arrow key, move the highlight to the number 7. This selects the date format, 03/19/68, the month

LESSON 37

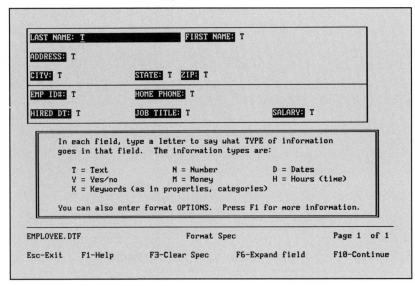

Figure 37.1: Format Spec

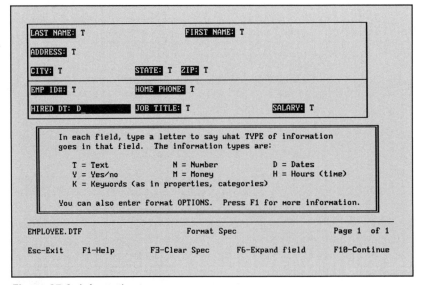

Figure 37.2: Information types

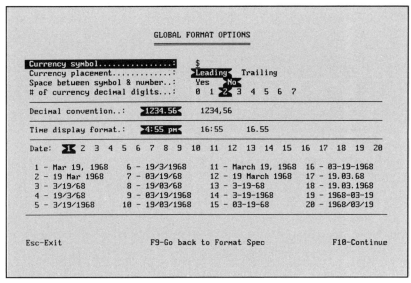

Figure 37.3: *Global Formatting options*

with two digits, the day with two digits and the year with two digits separated by slashes. By choosing this format, it will be easier to find specific dates when you search for date information later.

⑦ Press F10 to save the global formatting change you made. You are returned to the Q&A File menu. If you want to take a break now, press Esc to exit Q&A File. You are returned to the Q&A Main Menu.

Customizing Your Database: Creating a Field Template for Telephone Numbers

---

FEATURING

Field Template option
Customize a file option

YOU CAN CHANGE THE DESIGN OF YOUR DATABASE FORM any time. Q&A allows you to add and remove fields, move fields around the form, change the size of a field, and define information types. In addition to changing the layout of a form you can customize the form to suit your needs.

There are seven custom features you can set to make it easier and quicker when adding and updating records as well as reducing the number of errors when entering data.

Format values	Automatically capitalizes the text you enter into a field.
Restrict values	Either reminds you to enter information into a particular field, or requires you to enter information before you leave the form.
Set initial values	Allows you to fill the fields for each new record with information automatically. For example,

if you have many records that have the same information for an item called City, you can enter the city name with the Set initial values feature. Then, Q&A will display the city name in the City field for each new record you add to your database.

Field template

Lets you prepare a field for information such as a telephone number, social security number, or an account number. For example, with a telephone number field template, you can enter a phone number without parentheses or dashes such as 5089284572. Q&A will automatically enter the phone number as (508) 928-4572.

Speed up searches option

Lets you search and retrieve data much faster than usual.

Define custom help

Lets you design your own help messages, or special instructions, to further explain how to enter information in your database.

Change palette

Lets you change the colors on your Q&A File screens.

How to Create a Field Template

If you exited Q&A File in the previous lesson, read Lesson 33 on Starting Q&A File to load the program before starting this lesson.

In the EMPLOYEE database, let's explore the Field template custom feature to set up a field template for the Home Phone field.

This way, it will be easier for you to enter phone numbers when you add records to your database later.

① To create a field template from the Q&A File menu, press Enter to select the Design file option. The Design menu appears.

② Press C to highlight the Customize a file option.

③ Press Enter. Q&A prompts you to enter the name of the database file you want to customize.

④ Because the EMPLOYEE.DTF database file name is the one you want, simply press Enter to accept it. Q&A displays the Customize menu, shown in Figure 38.1. From this menu, you can prepare field templates with the Field template option.

⑤ Press T to highlight the Field template option. Then press Enter. The Field Template Spec appears on the screen.

⑥ Using the Tab key, move the cursor to the HOME PHONE field.

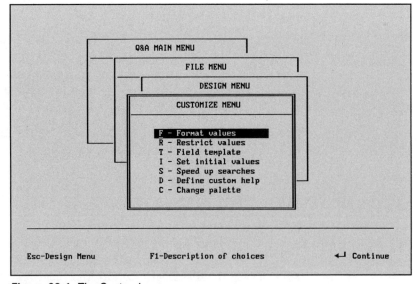

Figure 38.1: *The Customize menu*

⑦ Type **(###) ###-####**. (do not type the period.) The parentheses, the space, and the dash separate the ten-digit telephone number. The # (number symbol) represents a single number from 0 to 9. Compare your screen to the sample Field Template Spec shown in Figure 38.2.

⑧ Press F10 to save the field template. You are returned to the Customize menu.

⑨ Press Esc twice to return to the Q&A File menu.

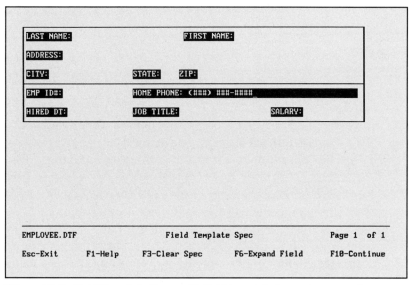

Figure 38.2: *Field Template Spec with field template for a phone number*

Inputting Forms

FEATURING

The Add data option

DATA MAY BE ADDED TO THE DATABASE AT ANY TIME after the file has been created. You can input forms in any order you like. There is no need to enter them in alphabetical or numerical order. Q&A File takes care of finding the information you want when you need it.

The Add data option displays a blank data-entry form so you can enter your data. The data-entry form contains the field labels and provides space for you to enter the data for each field. It's a little like having an electronic 3×5 card for each record. Q&A positions the cursor at the top of the form, ready for you to enter the data for the first field. As you enter data into each field, the cursor moves to the right. When you have completely entered the data for the field, press the Enter key to advance to the next field.

What happens if you make a mistake? No problem. Use the Backspace key to erase the error. Then type the correct information. Use the arrow keys, the Enter key, or the Tab key to move forward again.

When you have entered all of the data for one form or record, you must press F10. Q&A File clears the screen and provides you with a new, blank data-entry form for the next record. This process continues until you signal Q&A File that you have finished by pressing Shift-F10.

How to Input Forms

Let's get started with inputting forms in the EMPLOYEE database file. You will be entering data for eight records.

① To input forms, from the Q&A File menu, press A to highlight the Add data option and press Enter.

② Q&A File displays the last file that you worked on in the dialog box. In this case, it should be EMPLOYEE.DTF. If it is, then press Enter to accept it. If not, type the correct name now and press Enter. Q&A File displays a blank form with field names only. The cursor is positioned at the top of the screen next to the LAST NAME field.

③ Type **Jantzen** and press Enter.

④ Type **Samuel** and press Enter.

⑤ Type **24 Elmridge Street** and press Enter.

⑥ Type **Hudson** and press Enter.

⑦ Type **OH** and press Enter.

⑧ Type **44367** and press Enter.

⑨ Type **228950** and press Enter.

⑩ Type **2165556282** and press Enter. Notice that Q&A File enters the area code between the parentheses and the rest of the number appears before and after the dash. You don't have to enter the parentheses or dash because you set up a field template for the HOME PHONE field earlier.

⑪ Type **03/10/87** and press Enter. Notice that Q&A File enters the zero preceding the number three for the month. You don't have to enter preceding zeros for single digits because you set up a Global Formatting option for dates in the Hired Dt field earlier.

⑫ Type **Salesperson** and press Enter.

⑬ Type **45,000**. You have now completed entering the data for the first record. Compare your form on the screen to the form shown in Figure 39.1.

⑭ Press F10 to store the first record in your database. Q&A File clears the screen and displays a new blank form for the next record. Notice the Status line displays "New Record 2 of 2 Total Records 1" at the bottom of the screen.

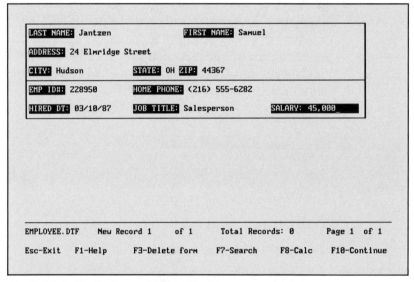

Figure 39.1: *The first record filled with data*

⑮ To add seven more records to your database, enter the following information. Be sure to press F10 after you fill in the form for each record.

LAST NAME: **Kelly**   FIRST NAME: **Sandra**

ADDRESS: **26 Oak Bend Terrace**

CITY: **Hartford** STATE: **CT** ZIP **06110**

EMP ID#: **249108** HOME PHONE: **(203) 247-3421**

HIRED DT: **02/25/86** JOB TITLE: **Salesperson**

SALARY: **47,000**

LAST NAME: **Forrester**   FIRST NAME: **Ridge**
ADDRESS: **5 Waverly Drive**
CITY: **Boston**   STATE: **MA** ZIP **02126**
EMP ID#: **247293** HOME PHONE: **(617) 682-4481**
HIRED DT: **05/07/88** JOB TITLE: **Designer**
SALARY: **50,000**

LAST NAME: **Olmsted**   FIRST NAME: **Marina**
ADDRESS: **36 E. 78th Street**
CITY: **New York** STATE: **NY** ZIP **10005**
EMP ID#: **457920** HOME PHONE: **(212) 436-2190**
HIRED DT: **03/20/87** JOB TITLE: **Salesperson**
SALARY: **49,500**

LAST NAME: **Blackwell**   FIRST NAME: **Donna**
ADDRESS: **220 Michigan Avenue**
CITY: **Washington** STATE: **DC** ZIP **20009**
EMP ID#: **332963** HOME PHONE: **(202) 651-2049**
HIRED DT: **12/22/87** JOB TITLE: **Designer**
SALARY: **48,000**

LAST NAME: **Jillian**   FIRST NAME: **Ross**
ADDRESS: **300 Pomona Boulevard**
CITY: **Malibu**   STATE: **CA** ZIP **93450**
EMP ID#: **263902** HOME PHONE: **(312) 668-9034**
HIRED DT: **06/15/90** JOB TITLE: **Salesperson**
SALARY: **47,000**

LAST NAME: **Zimmer**   FIRST NAME: **Jake**

ADDRESS: **50 Steerhorn Ranch**

CITY: **Dallas**   STATE: **TX** ZIP **75004**

EMP ID#: **273491** HOME PHONE: **(214) 784-3310**

HIRED DT: **08/02/89** JOB TITLE: **Salesperson**

SALARY: **35,000**

LAST NAME: **Atkins**   FIRST NAME: **Anna**

ADDRESS: **620 Eisenhower Boulevard**

CITY: **Tampa**   STATE: **FL** ZIP **33502**

EMP ID#: **238576** HOME PHONE: **(305) 227-8911**

HIRED DT: **10/12/87** JOB TITLE: **Salesperson**

SALARY: **35,000**

⑯ Press Shift-F10 to save all the records. You are presented with the Q&A File menu.

Retrieving Information from the Database

FEATURING

The Search option
The Retrieve Spec

ONCE DATA HAS BEEN STORED, A SINGLE PIECE OF information or a group of related data can be retrieved.

Q&A File provides a retrieve specification screen called the Retrieve Spec. This screen looks exactly like the form that you designed for your database which contained only field labels. You enter the specific information you want to search for into the Retrieve Spec. This instructs Q&A File to examine the entire database and to retrieve each record containing the information you want.

There are many ways to search and retrieve information. Use Exact Retrieval to search for information that exactly matches the retrieve specifications you enter. For example, you can search for an employee in your database who has a specific phone number. You enter that phone number in the HOME PHONE field to find the employee.

The Range Retrieval feature lets you search for numbers, letters, or words that have a meaning of larger, smaller or equal to associated with it. For example, you can search for a salary larger than $50,000.

The Number, Money, Date, or Time feature lets you search for number, money, date, or time values that have a meaning of larger, smaller or equal to associated with them. For example, you can search for a date later than 03/01/87.

You can use the Text or Keyword feature if you do not remember exactly how a piece of information is entered in a file, or if you want to find occurrences of specific pieces of information in your file. For example, you can retrieve all last names that begin with the letter K.

The Keyword Only feature is used to retrieve information found only in a keyword field. **Note:** A keyword field must first be set up (when you design the layout of your form) before you can use Keyword Only.

The Special Use Retrieval feature lets you retrieve information that is entered in one of the formats that represent Q&A File's information types. For example, you can retrieve all of the records that contain money, or a specific date.

You can retrieve information by searching in more than one field at one time. For example, you can tell Q&A File to search for all of the salespeople in the company or all of the employees whose salary is less than $50,000. Or, you could combine the two by searching for all of the salespeople who make less than $50,000.

With the employee records you have entered, you can use the Search/Update option to retrieve any information that you want to see in the EMPLOYEE database.

How to Retrieve Information from the Database

To demonstrate how quick and easy it is to retrieve information from the database, you will tell Q&A File to retrieve the record that contains the employee ID# 457920.

You will use the Exact Retrieval option to do this. To explore retrieving records further, let's search for all of the salespersons who were hired before 1988 by using the Date Search option. In addition, you will retrieve records from two fields by retrieving the names of all of the salespeople whose salary is less than $50,000.

① To perform an exact retrieval, begin by pressing S to highlight the Search/Update option on the Q&A File menu. Q&A File prompts you to enter the name of the database file that you want to use. The file name EMPLOYEE.DTF should appear at the bottom of the screen.

(2) Press Enter. Q&A File displays the Retrieve Spec screen, shown in Figure 40.1.

(3) Using the Tab key, move the cursor to the EMP ID# field.

(4) Type **457920**. This specifies to retrieve the record containing that particular employee ID number.

(5) Press F10. Q&A File retrieves and then displays the record containing the employee ID number that you specified.

(6) Press Esc to return to the Q&A File menu.

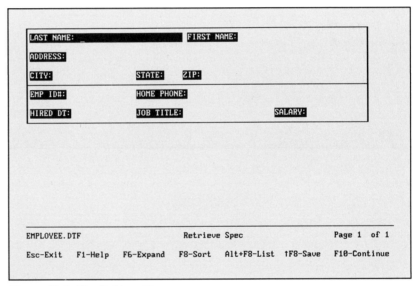

Figure 40.1: The Retrieve Spec screen

Performing a Date Retrieval

Now, let's do a date retrieval.

(1) To perform a date retrieval, begin by pressing S to highlight the Search/Update option on the Q&A File menu. Then press Enter.

(2) Using the Tab key, move the cursor to the HIRED DT field.

③ Type **<01/01/88**. The < (less than symbol) with a date specifies to retrieve records containing a hired date before January 1, 1988.

④ Press F10. Q&A File retrieves and displays the first record containing a hired date before January 1, 1988 that you specified.

⑤ When you have finished looking at the first record, press F10 to view the next record.

⑥ Use the F10 key to view each record one at a time. Q&A File retrieved five records. The number of records retrieved is displayed on the Status line at the bottom of the screen, for example, Form 5 of 5. You also can press F9 to see the previous record.

⑦ When you're finished looking at all of the records retrieved, press Esc to return to the Q&A File menu.

Performing a Retrieval By Searching in Two Fields

Now, let's search in two fields.

① Type **S** and then press Enter.

② To perform a retrieval by searching in two fields, begin by using the Tab key to move the cursor to the JOB TITLE field.

③ Type **salesperson**. This specifies to retrieve all records for employees who are salespeople.

④ Press the Tab key to move the cursor to the SALARY field.

⑤ Type **<50,000**. This specifies to retrieve all records for employees who are salespeople whose salary is less than $50,000.

⑥ Press F10. Q&A File retrieves and displays the first record containing a salesperson who makes less than $50,000.

⑦ When you have finished examining the first record, press F10 to view the next record. Notice the form number on the Status line reads Form 2 of 3. Q&A File retrieved three records.

⑧ Use the F10 key to view each record one at a time. When you're finished leafing through all of the records, press F9 twice to go back to Form 1.

Updating the Forms

FEATURING

The Update option
Alt-F6 (Table view) feature

Q&A FILE'S UPDATE FEATURE ALLOWS YOU TO MAKE changes to the contents of employee records. After you retrieve records from your database, you can make changes to information stored in the form. This is done by positioning the cursor in the field you want to change and entering new information.

Q&A File gives you two ways to update records retrieved with the Search option. You can edit one record at a time using the form that appears on the screen, or, you can edit the records in a list format called the Table view.

Let's give a raise to the salespeople who were hired before 1988 who make less than $50,000. Also, let's suppose that one of the salespeople, Samuel Jantzen, left the company. You will delete his record to remove his information from the database.

How to Update Forms

You will edit the first record using the form that appears on the screen. Then you will make the rest of the changes using the Table view feature.

(1) The first record displayed on your screen should contain a salesperson who makes less than $50,000. Let's press the Tab key to move the cursor to the SALARY field.

(2) Type **52,000**.

(3) Press F10 to view the next record.

(4) To see the records in a Table view, press the Alt-F6 (Table) function key. Observe that five fields are displayed across the table, as shown in Figure 41.1. A maximum of 17 records can be displayed in the table at one time. You can use the arrow keys to move around the table.

EMP ID#	HOME PHONE	HIRED DT	JOB TITLE	SALARY
228950	(216) 555-6282	03/10/87	Salesperson	52,000
249108	(203) 247-3421	02/25/86	Salesperson	47,000
273491	(214) 784-3310	08/02/87	Salesperson	35,000

EMPLOYEE.DTF   Retrieved record 2   of 3   Total records: 8

Esc-Exit   F1-Help   { ↓ ↑ → ← Home End PgUp PgDn }-Navigate   F10-Show form

Figure 41.1: *Table view of records*

(5) You can also edit the records in the Table view. To change the salary for the second record, type **53,000**.

(6) Press the Down-Arrow key to move the cursor to the salary amount for the third record.

(7) Type **54,000**.

⑧ Using the Left-Arrow key, move the cursor to the LAST NAME field at the beginning of the table. Notice how the table display changes as you press the Left-Arrow key. Now you should see the first five fields of your database.

⑨ Because Samuel Jantzen left the company, his record should be deleted. Press the Up-Arrow key twice to move the cursor to the record for Samuel Jantzen.

⑩ To delete the entire record, press the F3 (Delete) key. Q&A File asks you to confirm deleting the record.

⑪ Press the Left-Arrow key to move the highlight to Yes. This confirms the deletion.

⑫ Press Enter to remove the record. The information for Samuel Jantzen disppears.

⑬ Press F10 to show the form again.

⑭ Press Shift-F10 to save the changes that you made and return to the Q&A File menu.

If you want to take a break now, press Esc to exit Q&A File. You are returned to the Q&A Main Menu.

Sorting the Information

FEATURING

The Retrieve Spec
The Sort Spec

ONE OF THE MOST HELPFUL FEATURES OF Q&A FILE IS ITS
ability to sort records. You can easily rearrange the records so they
appear in virtually any order that is convenient for you—alphabetical,
numerical, or chronological.

The records for the EMPLOYEE database were purposely not
entered in any special order. You don't have to organize your information before entering the data in your database. What's nice about
Q&A File is that you can copy data from the paper forms just the way
it appears to enter it in a Q&A File database. Later you can sort the
information to suit your needs.

Q&A File lets you sort up to 9999 fields at one time. In practice,
sorting one or two fields at one time is customary.

How to Sort Information

If you exited Q&A File in the previous lesson, read Lesson 33 on
Starting Q&A File to load the program before starting this lesson.

Let's examine the Sort feature by sorting the employee records in
alphabetical order by last name.

LESSON 42

① To sort information, from the Q&A File menu, press S to highlight the Search/Update option. Q&A File displays the last file you worked on, EMPLOYEE.DTF.

② Press Enter. The Retrieve Spec appears.

③ Press F8. The Sort Spec appears, as shown in Figure 42.1.

④ Leave the cursor in the LAST NAME field. This is the field you want to sort.

⑤ Type **1AS** in the field. The 1 indicates that the LAST NAME field is the first (or primary) sort field you want to sort and the AS stands for ascending sort order.

⑥ Press F10. Q&A File sorts all of the records in alphabetical order according to last name. Note that the Atkins record is the first record in the database.

⑦ To view all of the records in sort order, press the Alt-F6 (Table) function key to see a table view of the records.

⑧ After you're finished looking at your records, press Esc to return to the Q&A File menu.

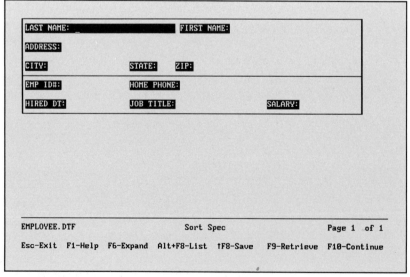

Figure 42.1: The Sort Spec

Printing the Database

FEATURING

The Print option
Design / Redesign a Print Spec

Q&A FILE LETS YOU PRINT THE INFORMATION IN A DATA-base in several ways. You can quickly print the record currently displayed on the screen simply by pressing Ctrl-F2, or you can print records using the Print option on the Q&A File menu. You can print the information onto prepared forms or plain paper.

There are two basic steps to print the records in a database: (1) set up the Fields Spec and (2) print the records.

Before you print any information from the database using the Print option, you must set up a print specification called the Print Spec. When you print database information on blank paper, the Print Spec lets you specify where you want to print each field on the paper.

How to Print the Database

In this lesson you will learn how to print all of the employee records, first by designing a Fields Spec and then printing the records from the Print Options screen.

Setting Up the Fields Spec

In the Fields Spec, you enter an X or a + (plus sign) next to each field. You type an **X** to print the field on a line and then move down to the beginning of the next line. You type a + to print the field, skip one space, and stay on the same line.

① To set up the Fields Spec, from the Q&A File menu, press P to highlight the Print option. Q&A File displays the last file you worked on, EMPLOYEE.DTF.

② Press Enter. Q&A File displays the Print menu, as shown in Figure 43.1.

③ Press Enter to select the Design/Redesign a spec option.

④ Q&A File prompts you to enter the name of the Print Spec you want to create. A Print Spec name can have a maximum of 30 characters and it may have spaces. At this point, an appropriate name would be empl forms (to stand for employee forms).

⑤ Type **empl forms** and press Enter. The Retrieve Spec appears. Notice Q&A File displays the message Retrieve Spec for EMPL FORMS at the bottom of the screen.

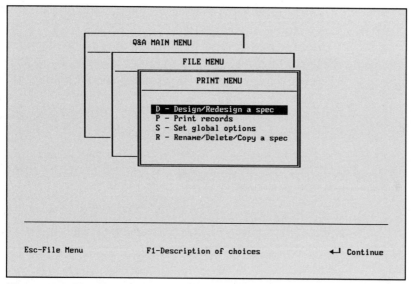

Figure 43.1: The Print menu

⑥ Press F10 to retrieve all of the forms or records in your database. The Fields Spec appears. Notice Q&A File displays the message "Fields Spec for EMPL FORMS" at the bottom of the screen. Now, you must tell Q&A File which fields you want to print and where you want them printed on the page.

⑦ In the LAST NAME field, type + (plus sign) and press Enter.

⑧ In the FIRST NAME field, type an **X** and press Enter.

⑨ Now that you have the idea, for the remaining fields in the Fields Spec, enter the following information:

ADDRESS	Type **X** and press Enter.
CITY	Type + (plus sign) and press Enter.
STATE	Type + (plus sign) and press Enter.
ZIP	Type **X** and press Enter.
EMP ID#	Type + (plus sign) and press Enter.
HOME PHONE	Type **X** and press Enter.
HIRED DT	Type + (plus sign) and press Enter.
JOB TITLE	Type + (plus sign) and press Enter.
SALARY	Type **X**.

⑩ After completing the Fields Spec information, compare your screen to the sample Fields Spec, shown in Figure 43.2.

*P*rinting the Records

Let's print all of the records in the employee database on plain white paper.

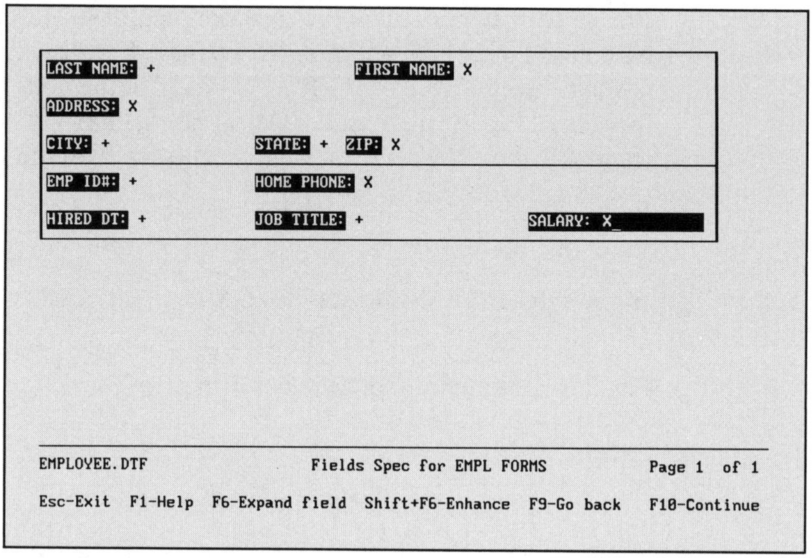

```
┌────────────────────────────────────────────────────────────────┐
│                                                                  │
│  ┌──────────────────────────────────────────────────────────┐  │
│  │ LAST NAME: +              FIRST NAME: X                    │  │
│  │ ADDRESS: X                                                 │  │
│  │ CITY: +          STATE: +  ZIP: X                          │  │
│  ├──────────────────────────────────────────────────────────┤  │
│  │ EMP ID#: +       HOME PHONE: X                             │  │
│  │ HIRED DT: +      JOB TITLE: +          SALARY: X_          │  │
│  └──────────────────────────────────────────────────────────┘  │
│                                                                  │
│                                                                  │
│                                                                  │
│                                                                  │
│  ────────────────────────────────────────────────────────────  │
│  EMPLOYEE.DTF         Fields Spec for EMPL FORMS     Page 1 of 1 │
│                                                                  │
│  Esc-Exit  F1-Help  F6-Expand field  Shift+F6-Enhance  F9-Go back   F10-Continue │
└────────────────────────────────────────────────────────────────┘
```

Figure 43.2: The Fields Spec

① To print the records, press F10. The Print Options screen appears, as shown in Figure 43.3.

② To print the records on plain white paper and make them look as if they are printed on a form, you can print the field labels as well as the field information. Notice the Print field labels option on the menu is set to No. This will print only the field information without the field labels. Press the Down-Arrow key to move the cursor to the Print field labels option. Press the Left-Arrow key to change the setting to Yes.

③ Note that the setting for the Number of records per page is two This will print only two records on a page. Because you are probably printing your records on 8 1/2" by 11" paper and the records consist of only five lines, you can fit three records per page. To change the setting to 3, press the Down-Arrow key to move the cursor to the Number of records per page option. Then type **3**.

④ Press F10 to continue to the next screen.

⑤ Q&A File prompts you to confirm printing the forms. The setting is Yes. Press Enter to print the forms. You are returned to the Print menu.

⑥ After the forms print, press Esc to return to the Q&A File menu.

If you want to take a break now, press Esc to exit Q&A File. You are returned to the Q&A Main Menu.

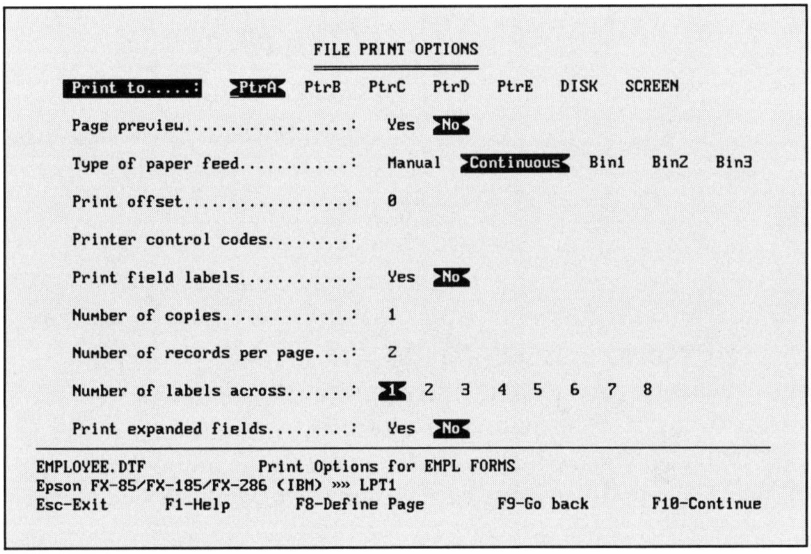

```
                           FILE PRINT OPTIONS
                           ═══════════════════
         Print to.....:    ▶PtrA◀  PtrB   PtrC   PtrD   PtrE   DISK   SCREEN

         Page preview.................:    Yes  ▶No◀

         Type of paper feed...........:    Manual  ▶Continuous◀  Bin1  Bin2  Bin3

         Print offset.................:    0

         Printer control codes........:

         Print field labels...........:    Yes  ▶No◀

         Number of copies.............:    1

         Number of records per page....:   2

         Number of labels across.......:   ▶1◀  2   3   4   5   6   7   8

         Print expanded fields........:    Yes  ▶No◀
     ───────────────────────────────────────────────────────────────────────
     EMPLOYEE.DTF          Print Options for EMPL FORMS
     Epson FX-85/FX-185/FX-286 (IBM) »» LPT1
     Esc-Exit      F1-Help      F8-Define Page       F9-Go back       F10-Continue
```

Figure 43.3: *Print Options screen*

Producing Form Letters Using the Mail-Merge Feature

FEATURING

The Merge field
The Alt-F7 (Merge field) function key

MERGING IS USED TO CREATE FORM LETTERS FOR MASS mailings, product announcements, customer letters, reports, invitations, and contribution solicitations. You also can merge a list of names and addresses to create invoices and mailing labels, and to fill in standard forms. You can even print addresses on envelopes with the Merge feature.

Q&A uses files from two programs to perform a merge, the document file from the Q&A Write program and the database file from the Q&A File program. The document file contains the basic letter, form, or invitation. Any information that stays constant is included in the document file. For example, the salutation, "Dear," and the letter closing, "Sincerely" never change.

Any information that does change is specified in the letter as a merge field. A merge field indicates where information will be inserted from the database file. The database file contains the merge fields which are inserted into the letter, such as the inside address, date, time, or place.

What is especially nice about Q&A's Mail-Merge feature is that you don't have to use any special merge codes in your document. You specify which database file you want to use and Q&A displays a list of the field labels contained in that database. Then, you simply choose the field label from the list that you want to insert in your letter. For example, suppose you want to create a mass mailing for a new product announcement. The database contains the names and addresses of the customers to whom you want to send announcements.

Q&A Write combines (or merges) the document with the information in the database file to produce each completed letter when you print the document.

There are three basic steps to produce merge letters in Q&A: (1) create a document in Q&A Write, (2) create a database in Q&A File, (3) print the merge letters in Q&A Write.

Suppose you want to announce a new product offered by your fictitious company, Office Designs. The easiest way to make this announcement is to do a mass mailing.

Just follow the steps in the lesson to write a typical product announcement and get some hands-on experience with the Mail-Merge in Q&A.

When you complete this lesson, you should have a good understanding of how to create simple Merge documents using Q&A Write and Q&A File, and you'll be ready to start merging documents of your own.

How to Produce Form Letters

If you exited Q&A File in the previous lesson, start with step 2 in this lesson.

In this part of the lesson you are shown how to create the Merge document in Q&A Write for the product announcement.

① To create your first Merge document, from the Q&A File menu, press Esc to exit Q&A File and to return to the Q&A Main Menu.

② Press W to select the Write option and then press Enter. You are presented with the Q&A Write menu.

LESSON 44

③ Press Enter to select the Type/Edit option. You are presented with a blank document.

④ Type today's date on line 1. Press Enter four times.

⑤ Press the Alt-F7 (Merge) function key. Q&A Write prompts you to enter the name of the database.

⑥ Type **employee** and press Enter. Q&A Write displays a list of the field labels in alphabetical order from your database on the right side of the screen, as shown in Figure 44.1.

⑦ Move the cursor to the FIRST NAME field and press Enter. Q&A automatically inserts a merge field into your document with asterisks before and after the field label.

⑧ Press the Spacebar. To insert the last name into your letter, press the Alt-F7 (Merge) function key again.

⑨ Move the cursor to the LAST NAME field and press Enter.

⑩ Press Enter again to move the cursor to the next line.

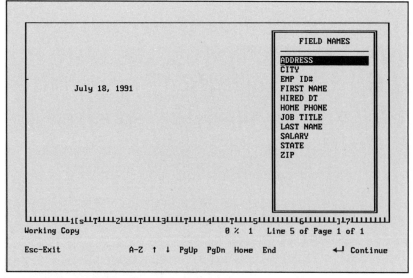

Figure 44.1: *Field labels from the database*

⑪ Using the Alt-F7 (Merge) function key, enter the following merge fields to complete the inside address in your letter.

ADDRESS	(on line 6)	Then press Enter.
CITY	(on line 7)	Then type a comma (,) and press the Spacebar.
STATE	(on line 7)	Then press the Spacebar twice.
ZIP	(on line 7)	Then press Enter twice.

⑫ Type **Dear** and press the Spacebar.

⑬ Press the Alt-F7 (Merge) function key and select the FIRST NAME field name.

⑭ Type a comma (,) and press Enter twice.

⑮ Type **THE PAPERLESS OFFICE IS HERE! OFFICE DESIGNS CAN NOW OFFER YOU A MULTI LEVEL FILING SYSTEM THAT IS RECESSED IN THE WALL. ORDER OUR FILING SYSTEM IN ANY COLOR TODAY!**

⑯ Press Enter. You have now completed the Merge document. Compare your document to the sample Merge fields in the document shown in Figure 44.2.

⑰ Press the Shift-F8 (Save) function key.

⑱ Type filesys **to name the document and press Enter.**

*P*rinting the Merge Letters

In this part of the lesson you learn how to insert the merge fields in the document using the EMPLOYEE.DTF database file. You are also shown how to print the Merge document in Q&A Write to produce personalized product announcements.

① Now that you have typed and saved a Merge document, you are ready to merge the document with the database information to create a personalized product announcement letter for every record you entered.

LESSON 44

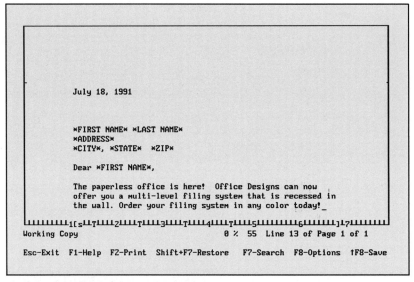

```
        July 18, 1991


        *FIRST NAME* *LAST NAME*
        *ADDRESS*
        *CITY*, *STATE*  *ZIP*

        Dear *FIRST NAME*,

        The paperless office is here!  Office Designs can now
        offer you a multi-level filing system that is recessed in
        the wall. Order your filing system in any color today!_

Luuuuuuu1[s²uTuu2uuuTuuu3uuuTuuu4uuuTuuu5uuuuuuu6uuuuuu]17uuuuuu
Working Copy                         0 % 55 Line 13 of Page 1 of 1

Esc-Exit  F1-Help  F2-Print  Shift+F7-Restore   F7-Search  F8-Options  ↑F8-Save
```

Figure 44.2: Merge fields in the document

② With your Merge document displayed, press F2 to display the Print Options screen, as shown in Figure 44.3. Note that the name of the database, EMPLOYEE.DTF, appears at the bottom of the Print Options screen and the name of the Merge document FILESYS appears below the database file name.

③ Press F10. The Retrieve Spec appears.

④ From the Retrieve Spec, you can select the records that you will use to produce the product announcements. In this case, let's choose to print merge letters for all of the records. Simply press F10 to retrieve all of the records in your database.

⑤ Q&A confirms the merging process with the message "FILE-SYS will be merged with 7 records from EMPLOYEE." Press F10 to print the merge letters. Q&A Write prints seven product announcements, one for each record in your EMPLOYEE database.

⑥ Press Esc to return to the Q&A Write menu.

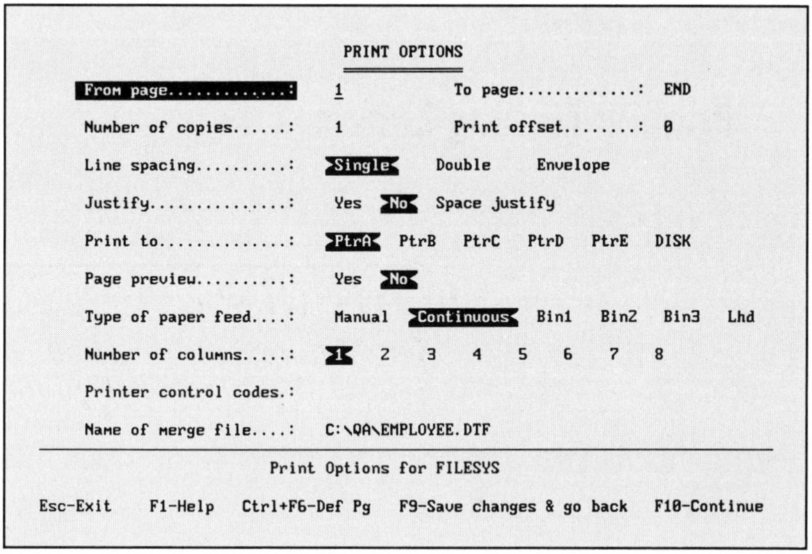

```
                              PRINT OPTIONS

         From page............:   1                 To page............:  END

         Number of copies......:   1                Print offset........:  0

         Line spacing..........:  >Single<   Double     Envelope

         Justify...............:  Yes  >No<  Space justify

         Print to..............:  >PtrA<  PtrB   PtrC    PtrD   PtrE   DISK

         Page preview..........:  Yes  >No<

         Type of paper feed....:  Manual  >Continuous<  Bin1   Bin2   Bin3   Lhd

         Number of columns.....:  >1<   2    3    4    5    6    7    8

         Printer control codes.:

         Name of merge file....:  C:\QA\EMPLOYEE.DTF
        ─────────────────────────────────────────────────────────────────────
                            Print Options for FILESYS

  Esc-Exit    F1-Help    Ctrl+F6-Def Pg    F9-Save changes & go back    F10-Continue
```

Figure 44.3: *The Print Options screen*

Printing Mailing Labels

FEATURING

The Mailing Labels option
The Alt-F7 (Merge field) function
key

Q&A PROVIDES A MAILING LABEL FEATURE THAT LETS you create, edit, and print mailing labels quickly and easily. To produce mailing labels you must use the Mailing labels option in the Q&A Write program and the names and addresses from a database in the Q&A File program.

Printing mailing labels is a two-step process: First, you set up the format of the mailing label. Then, you print the mailing labels using the information from your database.

Q&A Write provides many predefined mailing labels. Simply select the type of the mailing label you want to use. You can even choose from HP and HPII mailing labels. These are sheets of labels to be used only on Hewlett-Packard LaserJet and Hewlett-Packard LaserJet II printers. You can also print labels on pin fed continuous forms on a dot-matrix printer.

If you choose a predefined label to print on a dot-matrix or any other kind of printer, you may need to change the Blank lines at the top and the bottom options on the Mailing Labels Print Options screen.

*H*ow to Print Mailing Labels

Let's print mailing labels for the product announcements you created in the previous lesson. You can print them on label sheets that contain three labels across the page. If you don't have these label sheets, then select the label type that matches the size of the labels you have. If you don't have any labels for your printer, then print them on plain, white paper.

*S*etting Up the Format of a Mailing Label

Let's set up the format of a mailing label from the Q&A Write menu.

① Press M to select Mailing labels. Then press Enter. Q&A displays a list of label names in alphabetical order, shown in Figure 45.1, and prompts you to enter a label name.

② Move the cursor to the first label called Avery 5160 1″x 2 5/8″ HP.

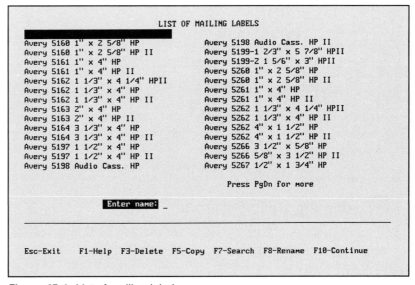

Figure 45.1: *List of mailing labels*

LESSON 45

③ Press the F5 (Copy) function key to select the label name from the list and copy the predefined label to a label format of your own.

④ The prompt "Copy to" appears at the bottom of the screen. A label name can have up to 32 characters and may contain spaces. An appropriate name would be file system. Let's abbreviate that name to filesys. Type **filesys** and press F10.

⑤ The label format you copied now appears on the left side of the screen, shown in Figure 45.2. Notice it contains generic name and address field labels.

⑥ Press F10 to save the label format.

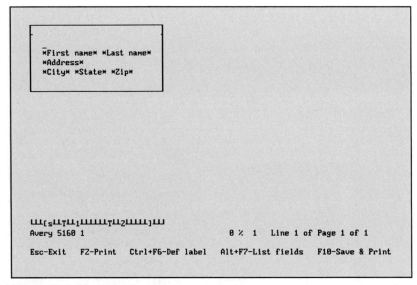

Figure 45.2: The Label format

Printing the Mailing Labels

Now you are ready to print the mailing labels on the label sheets or on plain white paper.

① The Mailing Label Print Options screen appears, as shown in Figure 45.3. Notice that the Number of labels across is set to 3 and the Space between labels is set at 1/8 of an inch. These are standard settings for the type of Avery label you selected.

② Press the Down-Arrow key to move the cursor to the Name of Q&A merge file field. Type **employee**.

③ Press F10 and the Retrieve Spec appears.

④ Press F10 to retrieve all of the records in your database. Q&A Write asks you to confirm merging the records with the label with the prompt "Avery 5160 1 will be merged with 7 records from EMPLOYEE."

⑤ Press Enter to confirm merging the records. Q&A Write and Q&A File merge the records. Then seven mailing labels are printed.

⑥ Press Shift-F8 to save the Label Spec.

⑦ Press Esc twice to return to the Q&A Main Menu.

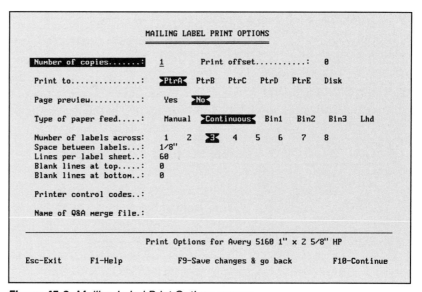

```
                      MAILING LABEL PRINT OPTIONS


  Number of copies.......:   1         Print offset...........:   0

  Print to...............:   PtrA   PtrB   PtrC   PtrD   PtrE   Disk

  Page preview...........:   Yes   No

  Type of paper feed.....:   Manual   Continuous   Bin1   Bin2   Bin3   Lhd

  Number of labels across:   1    2    3    4    5    6    7    8
  Space between labels...:   1/8"
  Lines per label sheet..:   60
  Blank lines at top.....:   0
  Blank lines at bottom..:   0

  Printer control codes..:

  Name of Q&A merge file.:

  ─────────────────────────────────────────────────────────────────
                  Print Options for Avery 5160 1" x 2 5/8" HP

  Esc-Exit      F1-Help          F9-Save changes & go back      F10-Continue
```

Figure 45.3: *Mailing Label Print Options screen*

Copying a Database: Backing Up the Database File to a Floppy Disk

---

FEATURING

The Copy option

TO ENSURE THE SAFETY OF THE DATABASE FILES YOU create in Q&A File, it is very important to back up your databases to a floppy disk. You can back up portions of the database or the entire database. For example, if you want to back up only the design of the database with the specs that you saved, you can use the Copy design only option. Or, if you want to copy selected records from one database to another, you can use the Copy selected records option.

To copy any part of a database, you must use the Copy option in the Q&A File menu. It is a simple procedure that doesn't take long to do and can save you a lot of time and work in the long run.

How to Copy a Database to a Floppy Disk

Let's copy the EMPLOYEE database file to a floppy disk with the Copy design only option. Remember, a copy of the database will be on the floppy disk as well as a copy remaining on the hard disk, therefore leaving you with two copies of the same file.

① Insert a formatted floppy disk in Drive A.

② From the Q&A Main menu, press F to select the File option. Then press Enter.

③ From the Q&A File menu, press C to select the Copy option. Then press Enter to accept the file name EMPLOYEE.DTF.

④ The Copy menu appears, shown in Figure 46.1.

⑤ Press Enter to select the Copy design only option.

⑥ The "Copy to" prompt appears in a dialog box at the bottom of the screen.

⑦ Using the Backspace key, erase C:\QA\.

⑧ Type **a:\employee**. This tells Q&A File that you want to copy the database to the floppy disk.

⑨ Press Enter. Q&A File copies the database from the hard disk to the floppy disk. Now you have a copy of your database on the floppy disk. The original database remains on the hard disk.

⑩ Press Esc twice to exit the Copy menu and return to the Q&A File menu.

⑪ Remove the diskette from Drive A.

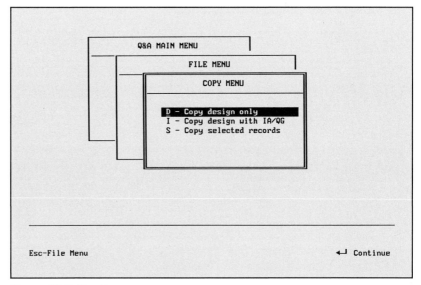

Figure 46.1: *The Copy menu*

Exiting Q&A File

FEATURING
The Exit option

WHEN YOU ARE FINISHED WORKING IN THE Q&A File program and you have saved all of your work, you can exit Q&A File.

How to Exit Q&A File

Press Esc to exit the Q&A File menu. You are returned to the Q&A Main Menu.

PART
FOUR

Q&A Report

Starting Q&A Report

FEATURING

Types of Reports

TO GET THE MOST "MILEAGE" OUT OF YOUR DATABASE, you'll need to master Q&A's built-in report generator, Q&A Report. This program lets you design as many as 200 types of reports based on the information from one database. You can also generate reports from more than one database. In Part Four, however, you will learn how to generate a report from only one database.

Typically, all of your Specs and options for each report are stored with your database. This allows you to create up to 200 reports per database. If you want to create quick, temporary reports without storing Specs and options, Q&A Report lets you produce *more* than 200 reports per database.

There are five major steps required to produce a professional-quality report in Q&A Report.

① You choose the type of report you want to generate.

② You tell Q&A Report to retrieve the records you want to use in the report.

③ Next you design the report by telling Q&A Report whether you want columns, rows, and calculations.

You can also enhance the report text by using bold, underline, italics, and by choosing various type fonts to change the appearance of the report.

④ You specify the print options you want to use, *i.e.,* single or double line spacing, and justify the text to print an even right margin. Once you select the print options, you can preview the report on the screen to see how the report looks before printing it.

⑤ You print the professional-quality report.

Basically, there are two major report types to choose from: columnar and cross tab. In a columnar report, you add the figures in each column and enter the totals at the bottom of each column. In a cross tab report, you can add the figures across each row and enter the totals at the ends of the rows as well as adding the figures in the columns and entering the totals at the bottom of each column. This way, you can cross-check your figures for accuracy by creating column totals as well as row totals.

In the lessons that follow, you will produce a simple columnar report. You will acquire enough hands-on experience to be ready to generate your own reports when you finish these lessons. These lessons assume that you already know how to create database files using Q&A File. If this is not the case, you will have to read Part Three, "Q&A File," and work through those lessons before continuing with Q&A Report.

Once you start the Q&A Report program, you will see the Q&A Report menu, which displays four menu options. These menu options are summarized in the following list:

Design/Redesign a report	Creates, edits and customizes reports.
Print a report	Prints a hard copy of the report.
Set global options	Changes the formatting and printing options for reports.
Rename/Delete/Copy	Lets you rename, delete, and copy reports.

The first menu option, Design/Redesign a report, appears highlighted or in a different color on the screen. To select an option from the

Q&A Report menu, you can (1) use the arrow keys, or (2) press the appropriate letter that appears to the left of the menu option. In the following lessons, you will select menu options using the second method.

How to Start Q&A Report

Now let's start the Report program.

① To start Q&A Report, from the Q&A Main menu, press R to move the highlight to the Report option.

② Press the Enter key. The Q&A Report menu appears on the screen, as shown in Figure 48.1.

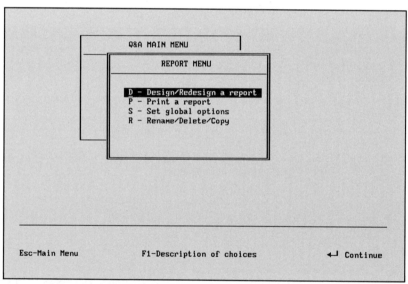

Figure 48.1: The Q&A Report menu

Creating a Columnar Report

FEATURING

The Report Type screen

THE FIRST STEP TOWARD CREATING ANY REPORT IN Q&A Report is to select the type of report that you want to generate. There are two types of reports listed in the Report Type screen: columnar and cross tab. Since you will create a simple columnar report in this lesson, let's examine the columnar report.

The columnar report consists of three main areas. The first area contains fields arranged in rows for each record. Each row contains a record. The second area consists of columns. Each column corresponds to a field in the record. The third area holds calculations such as subtotals and totals.

*H*ow to Create a Columnar Report

Let's create a columnar report that shows the salaries for all the employees at Office Designs. You can start by telling Q&A Report that you want to create a columnar report.

① From the Q&A Report menu, press Enter to select Design/ Redesign a report. Q&A Report prompts you to enter the name of the database file that you want to use to create this report.

② If Q&A Report displays the EMPLOYEE.DTF file name, simply press Enter to continue. Otherwise, type **employee** in the file name dialog box and then press Enter to continue.

③ Q&A Report asks you to enter the name of the new report. The name can have up to 31 characters. Type **salary** and press Enter. You are presented with the Report Type screen shown in Figure 49.1.

④ Press Enter to select Columnar report.

⑤ Q&A Report displays the Retrieve Spec for the columnar report.

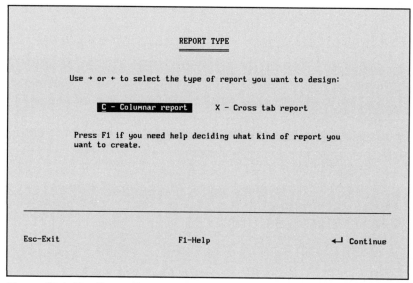

```
                          REPORT TYPE
                          ==========


          Use → or ← to select the type of report you want to design:


              C - Columnar report      X - Cross tab report


          Press F1 if you need help deciding what kind of report you
          want to create.




          _____


 Esc-Exit                        F1-Help                    ← Continue
```

Figure 49.1: The Report Type screen

Specifying Information to Use in the Report

FEATURING
The Retrieve Spec
The Column/Sort Spec

AFTER YOU SPECIFY THE TYPE OF REPORT THAT YOU want to create, the Retrieve Spec and the Column/Sort Spec specify the information that you want to use. First, you retrieve the records you want to use in the report and then you specify the way you want your report to look.

Retrieving records for a report is done the same way that you retrieve records in a database. Using Retrieve Spec, you can select *all* of the records from a database, or you can specify exactly which records you want.

How to Specify Information to Use in the Report

After you have specified what fields you want to use in the report, you must tell Q&A Report how to organize that information in a report format. This is done with the Column/Sort Spec screen. Column/Sort Spec lets you choose the column order of the fields you chose. Q&A Report lets you define up to 50 columns in a report. You must enter a number between 1 and 9999 next to each field that you want to include in the report. You can enter the field numbers in sequential order or you can number the fields in increments, such as 2,4,6 or 10,20,30. This also specifies the order in which the columns will appear. The lowest-numbered column will appear the farthest to the left.

*R*etrieving Records with the Retrieve Spec

Let's explore how to use the Retrieve Spec and the Column/Sort Spec in Q&A Report. Retrieving *all* of the employee records in the database is appropriate to create a report that show the salaries of all the employees at Office Designs. To arrange the format of the report, let's include the LAST NAME, FIRST NAME, and SALARY fields, thus giving us three fields in the report. Remember, each field appears as a column.

① At the end of Lesson 49, the Retrieve Spec for the columnar report was displayed on your screen, as shown in Figure 50.1.

② Press F10 to retrieve all records in the EMPLOYEE database.

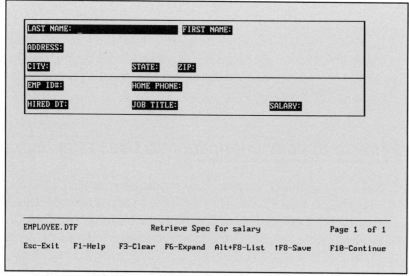

Figure 50.1: *The Retrieve Spec*

③ Q&A Report quickly retrieves the records. You are then presented with the Column/Sort Spec for the salary report.

*F*illing in the Column/Sort Spec

To start filling in the Column/Sort Spec screen, leave the cursor in the LAST NAME field.

① Type **1**. This indicates that the LAST NAME field is the first column in the report.

② Using the Enter key, move the cursor to the FIRST NAME field.

③ Type **2**. This indicates that the FIRST NAME field is the second column in the report.

④ Using the Enter key, move the cursor to the SALARY field.

⑤ Type **3**. This indicates that the SALARY field is the third column in the report. You have now completed telling Q&A Report which fields you want to include in the report and their column order, as shown in Figure 50.2.

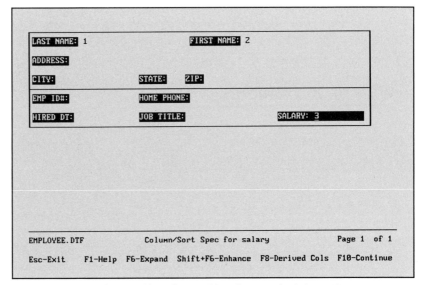

Figure 50.2: *The Column/Sort Spec with column order information*

LESSON 51

Sorting Information in the Report

FEATURING
The AS ascending sort code

AFTER YOU INDICATE THE ORDER OF THE FIELDS, YOU can sort the contents of the records in ascending or descending order. To do this, you simply enter a comma followed by a sort code. The comma separates the field number from the sort code. There are two sort codes: AS for ascending sort order and DS for descending sort order. With an ascending sort, Q&A Report ranks numbers and text in order from the lowest to the highest. For example, 0 to 9 and A through Z. With a descending sort, Q&A Report ranks numbers and text in order from highest to lowest. For example, 9 to 0 and Z through A.

How to Sort Records

Let's sort the LAST NAME field in ascending order. That way, Q&A Report will show the employee names in alphabetical order by last name.

① To sort the last names in alphabetical order, first use the Up-Arrow key to move the cursor to the LAST NAME field.

② Press the End key. This moves the cursor to the end of the field, after the number 1.

③ Type a comma (**,**).

④ Then type **AS**. This code stands for ascending sort order. You can enter the code in uppercase or lowercase.

⑤ Compare your screen to the sample Column/Sort Spec, shown in Figure 51.1.

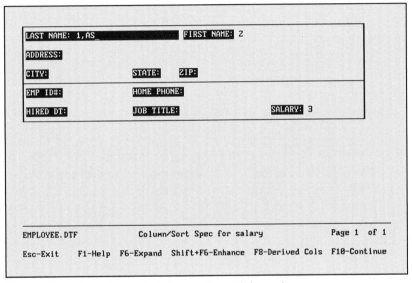

Figure 51.1: *The Column/Sort Spec with sort information*

Using Calculations in the Report

FEATURING
The T total code

ONE OF Q&A REPORT'S MOST POWERFUL FEATURES IS the ability to perform calculations on the columns in your reports. This produces a summary report complete with subtotals and the grand total.

For example, suppose you want to find out the total amount spent on salaries. Q&A Report lets you enter a formula that adds all of the salaries and puts the total amount at the bottom of the SALARY column.

How to Set Up Calculations

Let's set up a calculation to total the figures in the SALARY column.

① To total the figures in the SALARY column, use the Enter key to move the cursor to the SALARY field.

② Press the End key to move the cursor to the end of the field, after the number 3.

③ Type a comma (,).

④ Type **T**. The "T" is a code that stands for total. You can enter the code in uppercase or lowercase.

⑤ Compare your screen to the sample Column/Sort Spec shown in Figure 52.1. Notice the "T" code in the SALARY field.

If you want to take a break now, you can save the Report Spec by pressing F10 twice. Then press the Right-Arrow key to select No, and then press Enter. Press Esc to exit Q&A Report and return to the Q&A Main menu.

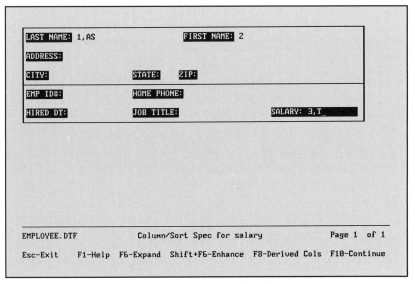

Figure 52.1: *The T (Total code) in the Column/Sort Spec screen*

Entering a New Heading in the Report

FEATURING

The TL total label code

SINCE THERE WILL BE A TOTAL AMOUNT IN THE THIRD column called SALARY, it is appropriate to enter a new heading at the end of the report in the same row as the total salary amount. Fortunately, Q&A Report allows you to enter a new heading. You do not need to use field names to enter headings for a report. For example, the new heading, Total Salary, would clarify the total salary amount in the last row of the report.

How to Enter a New Heading

When you want to enter a new heading for a grand total calculation it must appear in the first column of the report. The code that represents a new heading for a total amount is TL, for total label. Type the new heading enclosed in *parentheses*. Q&A Report will print only the information inside the parentheses in the first column at the bottom of the report.

In the salary report, the LAST NAME field is where you will enter the new heading information. Let's try it.

If you took a break earlier, you can start Q&A Report from the Q&A Main Menu by pressing R and then pressing Enter. Then select Design/Redesign a report from the Q&A Report menu. Type **employee** and press Enter. Select Salary and press Enter. Press F10. Now you can start with Step 2.

① To enter a new heading for the total salary amount at the bottom of the report, use the Up-Arrow key to move the cursor back to the LAST NAME field.

② Press the End key. This positions the cursor after the AS sort code.

③ Type a comma (,).

④ Type **TL (Total Salary)**. (Do not type the period.)

⑤ Q&A Report displays the message "Expand field: the number 1, AS, TL(Total Salary)" at the bottom of the screen. Because the codes fill the entire field, Q&A Report lets you expand the field to enter additional codes. Press the F6 (Expand) function key and the message will disappear. Compare your screen to the sample Column/Sort Spec, as shown in Figure 53.1.

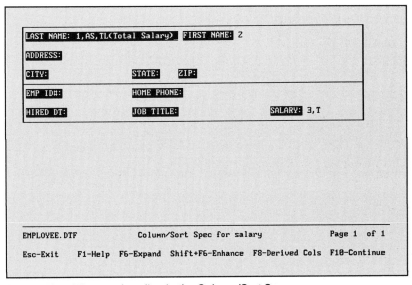

```
LAST NAME: 1,AS,TL(Total Salary)  FIRST NAME: 2

ADDRESS:

CITY:                  STATE:    ZIP:

EMP ID#:               HOME PHONE:

HIRED DT:              JOB TITLE:            SALARY: 3,T




EMPLOYEE.DTF          Column/Sort Spec for salary        Page 1  of 1

Esc-Exit    F1-Help  F6-Expand  Shift+F6-Enhance  F8-Derived Cols  F10-Continue
```

Figure 53.1: *The new heading in the Column/Sort Spec*

LESSON 54

Enhancing Text in the Report

FEATURING

The Shift-F6 (Enhance) function key

NOW THAT YOU KNOW HOW TO SPECIFY THE INFORMA-tion that you want to use in your report and how to enter formulas to perform calculations, you are ready to add the finishing touches to your report.

Q&A Report gives you several ways to enhance your reports by using the Text Enhancements and Fonts menu. You can apply **bold,** underline, ^{super}script, $_{sub}$script, *italics,* and ~~strikeout~~ to change the appearance of your text.

You also can change the fonts in your reports. Fonts are type faces that share a specific look and shape. For example, Helvetica has straight and simple characters, while Script has curvy and ornate characters. Each font has a name that you can select and apply to your report.

By applying an enhancement to the characters or changing the font, you can make the characters stand out from surrounding text or numbers.

How to Enhance Text in Your Report

Enhancing text in Q&A Report is a simple procedure. You position the cursor on the column number or code that represents the text you want to enhance. Q&A Report's Text Enhancements and Fonts menu lets you select the enhancement or font you want. Then you specify those characters that you want to enhance.

*E*nhancing Text with Bold

To draw attention to the Total Salary heading and the total salary amount in the last row, let's apply bold to the text and the numbers.

① To apply bold to the new heading, Total Salary, use the Right-Arrow key to move the cursor to the T in Total following the left parenthesis.

② Press the Shift-F6 (Enhance) function key. Q&A displays the Text Enhancements and Fonts menu, as shown in Figure 54.1.

③ Press Enter to select Bold.

④ Using the Right-Arrow key, highlight the words "Total Salary." Be sure not to highlight the parentheses.

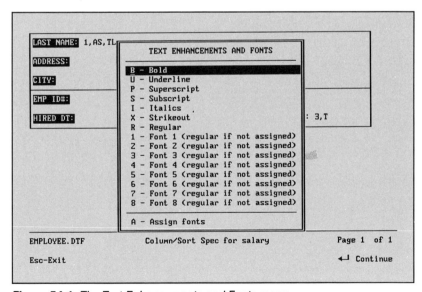

Figure 54.1: The Text Enhancements and Fonts menu

⑤ Press F10. The words "Total Salary" appear highlighted. The report's salary amount and Total Salary headings will appear in bold type when displayed with the Page Preview option, discussed later in Lesson 57, and when printed.

⑥ To apply bold to the total salary amount, use the Enter key to move the cursor to the SALARY field. Then press the Right-Arrow key twice to move the cursor to the letter T.

⑦ Press the Shift-F6 (Enhance) function key.

⑧ Press Enter to select Bold.

⑨ Press F10 to apply bold to the salary amount only. Notice the Bold indicator appears in the Status line next to EMPLOYEE.DTF when the cursor is on the enhanced text.

⑩ Compare your screen to the sample Column/Sort Spec screen, shown in Figure 54.2.

⑪ Press F10 to save the information you entered in the Retrieve Spec and Column/Sort Spec. You are presented with the Report Print Options screen.

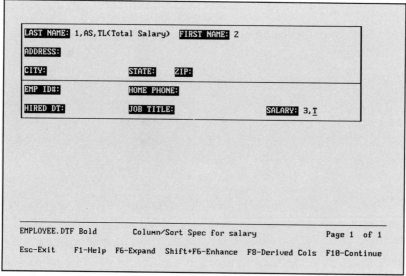

Figure 54.2: *The enhanced text in the Column/Sort Spec*

Adjusting Line Spacing

FEATURING

The Report Print options
The Double-Space option

NOW THAT YOU HAVE ADDED THE FINISHING TOUCHES TO your report, it is time to print it.

With Q&A Report you can specify several print options for printing reports. Furthermore, you can change any of the print options in the Report Print Options screen before you print your report.

Some of the print options that you can change include the type of paper feed, *i.e.,* manual or continuous, print the totals only, justify the text in the body of the report, and adjust line spacing.

Line spacing is the amount of white space between lines of text. You can specify either single or double-line spacing. Single-line spacing leaves a small of amount of white space between lines. Most reports are printed with single spacing. Double-line spacing leaves a larger amount of white space between lines, which is very helpful if you want to mark up the report, and it is easier to read.

How to Adjust Line Spacing

Let's change the line spacing for the salary report to double spacing. The double-spaced text in the report can be viewed later in Lesson 57 with the Page Preview option before you print the report.

① From the Report Print Options screen, press the Enter key until the cursor is on the Line spacing option.

② Press the Right-Arrow key to move the cursor to the Double option.

③ Compare your screen to the sample Report Print Options screen, shown in Figure 55.1.

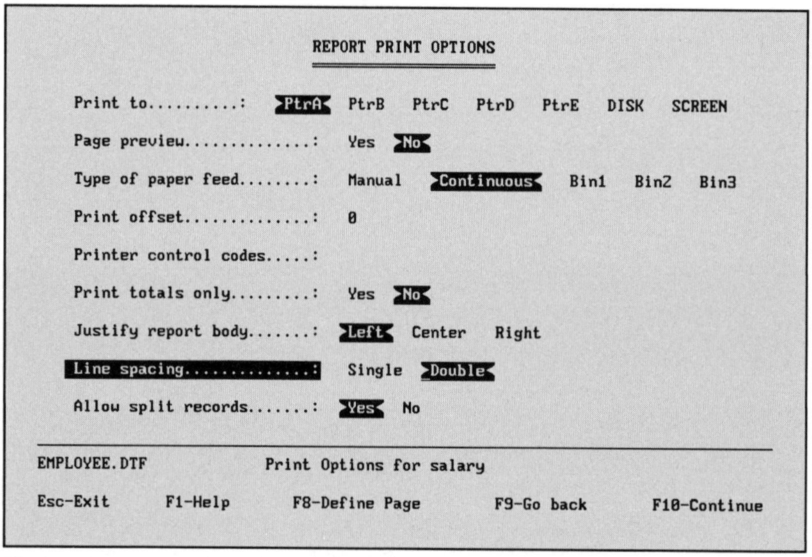

```
                        REPORT PRINT OPTIONS


       Print to.........:  ▸PtrA◂  PtrB   PtrC   PtrD   PtrE   DISK   SCREEN

       Page preview............:  Yes  ▸No◂

       Type of paper feed.......:  Manual  ▸Continuous◂  Bin1  Bin2  Bin3

       Print offset............:  0

       Printer control codes.....:

       Print totals only........:  Yes  ▸No◂

       Justify report body.......:  ▸Left◂  Center  Right

       Line spacing............:  Single  ▸Double◂

       Allow split records.......:  ▸Yes◂  No
  ─────────────────────────────────────────────────────────────────
  EMPLOYEE.DTF          Print Options for salary

  Esc-Exit      F1-Help      F8-Define Page      F9-Go back      F10-Continue
```

Figure 55.1: _Line spacing in the Report Print Options screen_

Adding Headers and Footers

FEATURING

The F8 (Define Page) function key

A HEADER IS TEXT THAT APPEARS AT THE TOP OF EVERY page of a report and a footer is text that appears at the bottom of every page. You can use a header and footer to repeat the title of the report, number pages automatically, and enter the date and time.

When you enter the header and footer text, Q&A Report will print the header and footer within the top and bottom margins of the report. Q&A Report lets you enter up to three lines of text for a header and a footer.

The Define Page screen is where you enter header and footer information as well as where you change several page size options before you print the report. You can change the page width and length, margins, and characters per inch for the size of the text in your report.

How to Add Headers and Footers to Your Report

Let's set up a header to enter a title at the top of the report. "Salary Report" is an appropriate title. You will also enter the date at the top of your report. Let's also set up a footer to number the pages automatically. The header and footer text can be viewed later in Lesson 57 with the Page Preview option before you print the report.

① From the Report Print Options screen, press the F8 (Define Page) function key. You are presented with the Define Page screen.

② Using the Enter key, move the cursor to the first line of the Header option labeled "1:" at the bottom of the screen. Notice there are three lines available for you to type the header text.

You can align the header and footer text left, right, and center by entering an **!** (exclamation point) to indicate where the text should appear. To enter the date, you must type a special function, **@DATE**, followed by a numeric code that specifies how the date will be displayed. Refer to your Q&A documentation for a list of all of the date display formats. To specify automatic page numbering, you type a number sign (*#*).

③ To enter the title for the report, and the date and time, type **Salary Report!!@DATE(1)**. (Do not type this period.) The first exclamation point aligns the title to the left and the second exclamation point aligns the date to the right. The @DATE(1) function inserts today's date in the format month, day, and year.

④ Press the Enter key three times to move the cursor to the first line of the Footer option labeled "1:."

⑤ To specify automatic page numbering, type **!Page #!**. (Do not type this period.) Be sure to enter a space between the word "page " and the # (number sign). This centers the page numbers in your report.

⑥ Compare your screen to the sample Define Page screen, shown in Figure 56.1.

⑦ Press F9 to return to the Report Print Options screen.

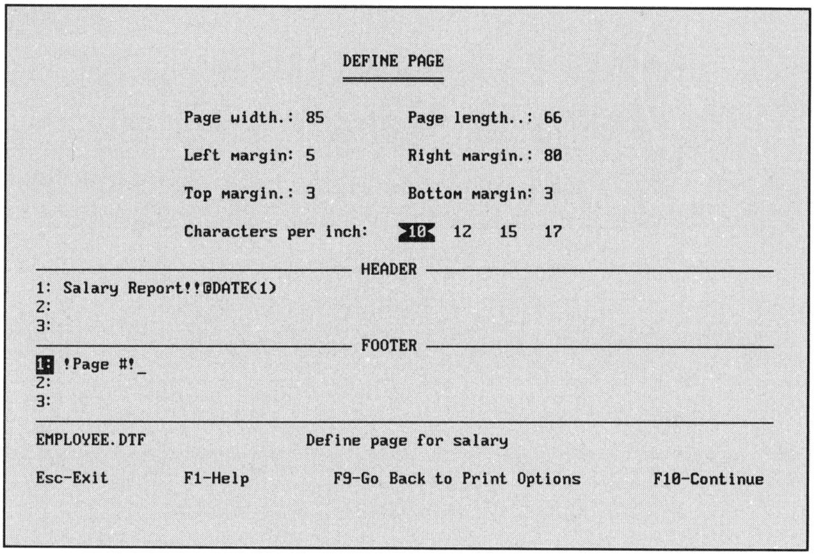

```
                              DEFINE PAGE
                              ==========

                Page width.: 85        Page length..: 66

                Left margin: 5         Right margin.: 80

                Top margin.: 3         Bottom margin: 3

                Characters per inch:   ▓10▓  12   15   17
─────────────────────────────── HEADER ───────────────────────────────
1: Salary Report!!@DATE(1)
2:
3:
─────────────────────────────── FOOTER ───────────────────────────────
▓1▓ !Page #!_
2:
3:
───────────────────────────────────────────────────────────────────────
EMPLOYEE.DTF              Define page for salary

Esc-Exit        F1-Help        F9-Go Back to Print Options      F10-Continue
```

Figure 56.1: *Header and footer text in the Define Page screen*

Previewing the Report

FEATURING

The Page Preview option

BEFORE YOU PRINT YOUR REPORT, YOU CAN SEE HOW IT will look by previewing it on your screen. The Page Preview option in the Report Print Options screen works the same way as the Page Preview option in Q&A Write. Viewing the report on the screen is a good way to determine if any changes are necessary before printing a final copy of the report.

The Page Preview option displays a miniature version of the formatted pages of the report on your screen. You can see the placement and appearance of headers and footers, page numbers, the report title, the date, text enhancements, margins, and line spacing. However, you cannot edit or format your report in Page Preview mode. You must switch back to the Column/Sort Spec, the Report Print Options screen, and the Define Page screen to make any further changes.

*H*ow to Use Page Preview

Let's take a look at the report with Page Preview to see how the report will look when it prints out.

① From the Report Print Options screen, press the Enter key to move the cursor to the Page Preview option.

② Press the Left-Arrow key to move the cursor to Yes.

③ Press F10. Q&A tells you that your design has been saved and also asks you if you want to print the report. Press Enter to select the Yes option. You are presented with the Page Preview screen, shown in Figure 57.1.

④ Press + (plus) to zoom in and enlarge the report. Press the Right-Arrow key until you can see the date at the top right of the report. Notice the column headings are underlined and a double underline appears at the bottom of each column. The report is sorted alphabetically by last name. The Total Salary heading that is bolded appears at the bottom-left in the report. The total salary amount also appears bold. Press PgDn twice to see the page number at the bottom-center of the report.

⑤ Press − (minus) to zoom out and view a full page of your report.

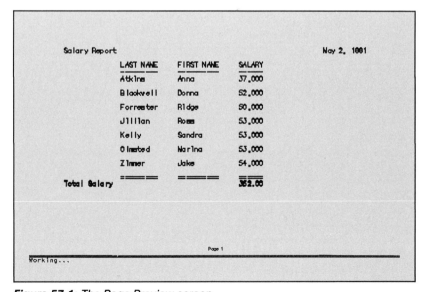

Figure 57.1: *The Page Preview screen*

⑥ Press F2 to exit the Page Preview screen. You are returned to the Report Print Options screen.

⑦ To set the Page Preview option to No, press the Down-Arrow key once to select Page Preview, and then press the Right-Arrow key. Now you are ready to print your report.

Printing the Report

FEATURING
Saving the Report Spec

ONCE YOU HAVE VIEWED THE REPORT WITH THE PAGE Preview option, you can either make any necessary changes or print the report. Just before you print the report, Q&A Report tells you that the report you defined has been saved. Then you can either print the report immediately or return to the Report menu and print the report later.

What's nice about Q&A Report saving your defined Report Spec is that you won't have to repeat the process to print another salary report in the future. When you want to print another salary report, you simply select Print a report from the Report menu, recall the defined report by its name, select the records you want to include in the report, and then print it.

How to Print the Report

Let's print the salary report now and see how it looks on paper.

① From the Report Print Options screen, press F10. Q&A tells you that the defined report has been saved.

② Press Enter to select Yes. This prints the report.

LESSON 58

③ After the report prints out, you are returned to the Report
menu. Compare your report to the sample Salary Report,
shown in Figure 58.1.

```
Salary Report
                LAST NAME      FIRST NAME      SALARY
                ---------      ----------      ------
                Atkins         Anna            37,000

                Blackwell      Donna           52,000

                Forrester      Ridge           50,000

                Jillian        Ross            53,000

                Kelly          Sandra          53,000

                Olmsted        Marina          53,000

                Zimmer         Jake            54,000

                =========      ==========      ======
Total Salary                                   352.00
```

Figure 58.1: The Salary Report

Exiting Q&A Report

FEATURING
The Esc key

WHEN YOU'RE FINISHED CREATING AND PRINTING reports in Q&A Report, you can exit the program very easily.

Now that you have printed your columnar report, let's exit the program.

How to Exit Q&A Report

From the Q&A Report Menu, press Esc to return to the Q&A Main Menu.

PART

FIVE

The Assistant

L ESSON 60

Starting the Assistant

FEATURING
Artificial Intelligence

THE ASSISTANT IS Q&A'S ARTIFICIAL INTELLIGENCE PRO-
gram that is specifically designed for the beginner. With it you can find
and retrieve information from a database using English questions
instead of having to use Q&A File and Q&A Report commands.

The phrase "artificial intelligence" is used to describe programs
that enable computers to play chess, prove theories, recognize pat-
terns, or do anything requiring reasoning or learning. Communicat-
ing by means of a human language such as English, rather than a
computer language, is one of the major goals accomplished by an artificial intelligence program like the Assistant.

If you are new to the Assistant and feel somewhat intimidated by
it, this chapter will help you to master the basics quickly. You may use
as much or as little of the Assistant as you wish. Some Q&A users will
find no reason to learn the Assistant portion of the Q&A program.

Other users may experiment with the Assistant in small ways to
query information from their databases, and then gradually try more
ambitious projects as their knowledge of the Assistant's procedures
and abilities grows. Still others, with previous Q&A experience, may
begin using the Assistant immediately for designing custom queries.

The Assistant is a valuable tool to increase productivity because,
among other virtues, it sharpens your own thinking. As you become
familiar with the Assistant, you will find that it may sharpen your
enjoyment, as well. Using the Assistant, however, does require some

previous Q&A experience. If you haven't used Q&A File and Q&A Report before, please read Part Three and Part Four and work through the lessons before continuing any further with Part Five.

Q&A provides two ways to work with the Assistant: these are the Intelligent Assistant and the Query Guide. The Intelligent Assistant, sometimes referred to as the IA, uses a natural English language to enter requests into Q&A just as though you were speaking to a human assistant. It contains 600 words and phrases, and it also knows the words used as field labels in your database. You can teach the IA new words; for example, medical, legal, or other special terms that you use in your business. You can ask questions in the IA to compare different parts of your database such as "Whose hired date comes between Atkins and Forrester?" You can also ask immediate follow-up questions without redefining the subject of the query, for instance, "What are their salaries?" The IA also permits you to create ad-hoc reports quickly and easily.

The Query Guide is a new feature in Q&A Release 4.0. It produces the same results as the Intelligent Assistant; however, it steps you through the process of building more accurate requests to get the results you want more precisely.

The IA and the Query Guide are similar in the following ways: they are used to retrieve, sort, and update records, perform calculations, and generate reports; they require teaching the Assistant all about your database; and they use English sentences to build requests. The IA and the Query Guide both allow you to perform tasks that can be done in Q&A File and Q&A Report, as well as to perform tasks that cannot be done in Q&A File and Q&A Report.

The IA and the Query Guide are different when you build a request. When you use the IA to build a request, it can be time-consuming because the IA might not understand your query immediately. If this happens, the IA stops processing your query and asks you to clarify certain words and phrases in order to process your request. When you build a request with the Query Guide, it is easier and faster because you can choose sentence fragments listed in the Query Guide menus. The sentence fragments are easy to understand. For example, you select the fragment "Find" from the Query menu to search for records in your database. In another example, you select the fragment "ALL the records" to search for all of the records in your database.

The Intelligent Assistant and the Query Guide are accessed from the Assistant menu. The Assistant menu displays the following five menu options:

Get acquainted	Gives you basic information on what the Intelligent Assistant is and what it can do.
Teach me about your database	Provides lessons that will teach the Intelligent Assistant the words you will use when referring to the information in your database.
Ask me to do something	Uses lessons you set up in the Intelligent Assistant to retrieve records, update records, perform calculations, and create reports.
Query Guide	Helps you build requests using predefined sentences to retrieve records, update records, perform calculations, and create reports.
Teach Query Guide	Teaches the Query Guide all about the information in your database.

How to Start the Assistant

Let's start the Assistant and examine the Assistant menu.

① To start the Assistant, from the Q&A Main Menu, press A to move the highlight to the Assistant.

② Press Enter. You are presented with the Assistant menu, shown in Figure 60.1.

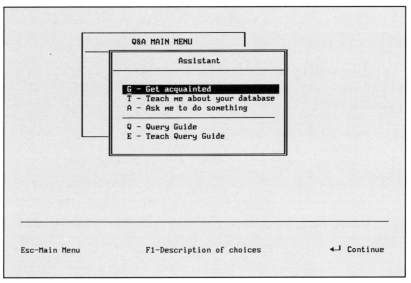

Figure 60.1: *The Assistant menu*

Teaching the Query Guide

FEATURING
The Teach Query Guide Spec
The F5 (Select All) function key

THE GREATEST STRENGTH OF THE ASSISTANT IS THE Query Guide. It teaches you how to set up questions using the English language to find and retrieve information from your Q&A File database.

The Query Guide is very user-friendly because it has an expanded vocabulary that helps the Assistant in understanding requests, and eliminates the need for rephrasing. It is menu-driven and contains many prompts for you to enter information, instead of requiring the Query Guide to guess at what information you might enter.

The first step toward using the Query Guide is to teach it all about your database. You use the Teach Query Guide option to do this by indicating those fields that you want to include. Q&A enters the letter Q next to each field that you want the Query Guide to learn. The field labels and the contents of the records are first reviewed by Q&A and then stored in the Query Builder. Then, the Query Builder will contain an index of all of your field labels and the information contained in all of the records in your database.

To give the lessons some context, let's retrieve information from the employee database used earlier in Part Three, "Q&A File." Let's teach the Query Guide what your employee database is about and then use it to retrieve information.

*T*eaching the Query Guide

We will teach the Query Guide to include all of the fields in your database.

① From the Assistant menu, press E to move the highlight to the Teach Query Guide option.

② Press Enter. Q&A prompts you to enter the name of the database file you want to use.

③ Type **employee** and press Enter. Q&A displays the Teach Query Guide Spec. Notice that the Help screen appears below the Teach Query Guide Spec.

④ Press the F5 (Select All) function key. Q&A selects all of the fields in the database by entering the letter Q next to each field label. Compare your screen to the sample Teach Query Guide Spec, shown in Figure 61.1.

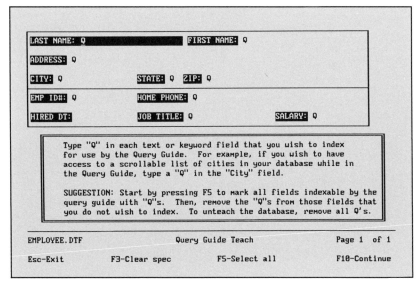

Figure 61.1: *The Teach Query Guide Spec*

⑤ Press F10. Q&A reviews the contents of the database and displays a dialog box showing the percentage of the database it has reviewed. When Q&A finishes reviewing the database, you are returned to the Assistant menu. All of the field labels and the contents of the records are now stored in the Query Builder.

Retrieving Records with the Query Guide

FEATURING

The F3 (Restart) function key

THE NEXT STEP IN USING THE QUERY GUIDE IS TO actually tell it what you want to do. For example, you can have it retrieve records, sort records, update records, perform calculations, and create reports. Of course, you can perform all of these tasks using Q&A File and Q&A Report, but the Query Guide combines the programs and lets you make requests in English sentences instead of having to enter commands.

The Query Guide contains fragmented sentences or phrases from which you can build your own requests. You select these fragments from the Query Guide menu that displays the following six menu options:

Find	Retrieves, sorts, adds, and updates records.
Produce a report showing the	Creates columnar reports.
Count	Counts the number of records in the database.
Summarize the data by	Creates summary reports.
Run	Prints a predefined report.
Cross-tabulate	Creates cross tab reports.

Simply select the task from the menu that you want to perform and then Q&A displays the English phrase on the screen. As you are building the request, you can view it on the screen. You continue to build the request until you have entered all of the phrases necessary to complete the English sentence. If you make a mistake, use the F3 (Restart) function key to erase the phrase that you entered and start again.

Q&A's Query Guide contains several menus to step you through each portion of the request you want to make. Each Query Guide menu contains a list of tasks. Each time you select a task from the menu you are adding to the English sentence. Q&A uses this sentence to request the information that you want to retrieve from the database.

Once you retrieve the information that you want using the Query Guide, Q&A displays the same screens used in the Q&A File program. You will see familiar screens that contain records.

How to Retrieve Records Using the Query Guide

Your first attempt at using the Query Guide will be to build a request that retrieves all of the records in the employee database. Let's see how this feature works.

1. To begin retrieving records, from the Assistant menu, press Q to select Query Guide.

2. Press Enter. Q&A displays the EMPLOYEE.DTF database file name in the dialog box.

3. Press Enter. Q&A displays the Query Guide screen. Notice the Ask box at the top of the screen and the Query Guide menu below it, shown in Figure 62.1.

4. Press Enter to select the Find option. Q&A displays the word Find in the Ask box at the top of the screen and the Find menu below it, as shown in Figure 62.2.

5. Press A to select ALL the records option. Then press Enter. Q&A displays the phrase "Find ALL the records" in the Ask box.

⑥ The last step in building the request is to end the sentence in the Ask box with a period, just as you would put a period at the end of a sentence. The first command on the menu is .-. where the first period indicates that you can press the period key to select the command instead of pressing the Enter key. A hyphen separates the two periods. The second period tells you that a period will be added to the end of the sentence. Press Enter. A period appears at the end of the sentence in the Ask box. Q&A flashes the message "Searching" in the lower left corner of the screen while it searches for all the records.

⑦ The first record displays on the screen and looks just like the screen displayed in Q&A File when you retrieve records. Using the F10 function key, view each record. You can also use the F9 function key, just as in Q&A file, to view the previous record.

⑧ When you have finished viewing the records, press Esc to return to the Query Guide menu.

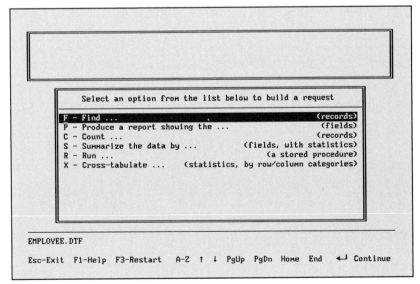

Figure 62.1: *The Query Guide screen*

LESSON 62

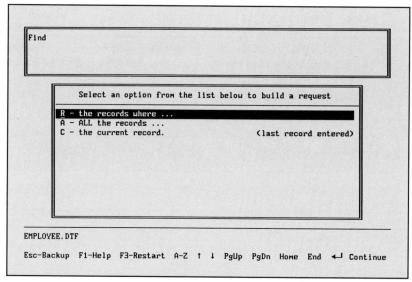

Figure 62.2: *The Find menu in the Query Guide*

Sorting Records with the Query Guide

FEATURING
The Query Guide

NOW THAT YOU KNOW HOW TO RETRIEVE RECORDS WITH
the Query Guide, let's examine how to sort the records with the Query
Guide.

There are three steps for sorting records with the Query Guide.
First, you must select the Find option from the Query Guide menu to
ask Q&A to retrieve the records. Second, you select the Sort option on
the Query Guide menu to sort the records. To sort the records, you
don't have to enter the AS or DS codes to sort in ascending or
descending order, as you did in the Q&A File program. The third and
last step is to specify which fields you want to sort.

How to Sort Records Using the Query Guide

Suppose you want to see the records for all of the employees at
Office Designs in alphabetical order by last name. Let's examine how
that works.

1. To begin sorting records, from the Query Guide menu, press
   Enter to select the "Find" option.

2. Press A to select the "ALL the records" option. Then press
   Enter.

③ From the Query Guide menu, press S to select the Sorted by option. Then press Enter. Q&A displays a list of the fields in the employee database.

④ From the Select a field list, press the Down-Arrow key to move the cursor to the LAST NAME field, as shown in Figure 63.1.

⑤ Press Enter. Q&A shows the sentence "Find ALL the records sorted by LAST NAME" in the Ask box at the top of the screen.

⑥ Press the Down-Arrow key twice to select the .-. option. This option enters a period at the end of the sentence in the Ask box.

⑦ Press Enter to add a period to the end of the sentence and execute the Sort command.

⑧ The first record containing the Atkins employee information displays on the screen and looks just like the screen displayed in Q&A File when you retrieve and sort records. Using the

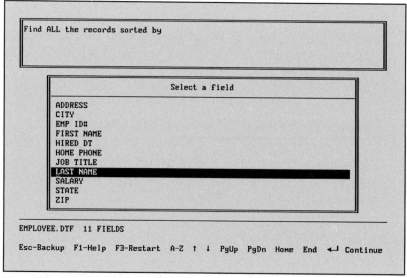

Figure 63.1: *The Select a Field list*

F10 key, view each record sorted in alphabetical order by last name. You can also use the F9 key, just as in Q&A file, to view the previous record.

(9) When you have finished viewing the records, press Esc to return to the Query Guide menu.

If you want to take a break now, press Esc to exit the Query Guide menu and press Esc again to exit the Assistant. You are returned to the Q&A Main Menu.

Creating a Report with the Query Guide

FEATURING
Creating a report

SO FAR, YOU'VE LEARNED HOW TO RETRIEVE AND SORT records with the Query Guide. Now that you've got the idea, let's create a report using the Query Guide.

You don't have to enter any special codes to set up the report, as you did in Q&A Report. You just select the report options from the Query Guide menu and Q&A will generate the report based on the requests you make.

There are three major steps involved in creating a report. They are: (1) specifying the fields that you want in the report, and the order in which they will appear; (2) retrieving the records you want to include in the report, and (3) sorting the records.

After you build the request to create the report, Q&A will display the report on the screen. You can even move around the report to view the information from top to bottom.

How to Create a Report Using the Query Guide

If you exited the Assistant in the previous lesson, from the Q&A Main Menu, press A and then press Enter to load the Assistant program into your computer's memory. From the Assistant menu, press Q to select Query Guide and then press Enter. Type **employee** and press Enter. Q&A displays the Query Guide screen.

Suppose you want to create a simple report that shows when each employee was hired at Office Designs. The report will contain the employee's first and last name, the job title, and the date hired, and will be sorted by the date hired. Let's use the Query Guide to build a request for generating this report.

① To begin creating a report, press P from the Query Guide menu, to select the "Produce a report showing the" option. Then press Enter.

② Q&A displays a list of all the fields in your database. Using the Down-Arrow key, move the cursor to the LAST NAME field.

③ Press Enter. Q&A displays a menu containing conditions for selecting additional fields. The "&-and" option lets you select additional fields.

④ Press Enter to select the "&-and" option.

⑤ To enter additional fields, repeat Steps 2 through 4 to select the following:

FIRST NAME

JOB TITLE

HIRED DT

⑥ From the Query Guide menu, press F to select "From (records)". Then press Enter. This option retrieves the records.

⑦ Press A to select "ALL the records." Then press Enter.

⑧ From the Query Guide menu, press S to select the "Sorted by" option. Then press Enter. Q&A displays a list of the field labels in the employee database.

⑨ From the "Select a field" list, press the Down-Arrow key to move the cursor to the HIRED DT field.

⑩ Press the Down-Arrow key twice to select the .-. option. This will insert a period at the end of the sentence in the Ask box and execute the request.

⑪ Press Enter to generate the report.

⑫ Q&A displays the entire request in the Ask box at the top of the screen and the report below it, as shown in Figure 64.1.

⑬ Using the Up-Arrow and Down-Arrow keys, move around the report to view all of the information. Notice the hired dates are in ascending order.

⑭ When you have finished viewing the report, press F10 to return to the Query Guide menu.

```
┌────────────────────────────────────────────────────────────────────────┐
│ ┌──────────────────────────────────────────────────────────────────┐   │
│ │Produce a report showing the LAST NAME and the FIRST NAME and the JOB TITLE│ │
│ │and the HIRED DT from ALL the records sorted by HIRED DT.          │   │
│ └──────────────────────────────────────────────────────────────────┘   │
│                                                                          │
│  LAST NAME      FIRST NAME      JOB TITLE      HIRED DT                   │
│  ---------      ----------      ---------      --------                   │
│  Kelly          Sandra          Salesperson    02/25/86                   │
│                                                                          │
│  Olmsted        Marina          Salesperson    03/20/87                   │
│                                                                          │
│  Zimmer         Jake            Salesperson    08/02/87                   │
│                                                                          │
│  Atkins         Anna            Designer       10/12/87                   │
│                                                                          │
│  Blackwell      Donna           Designer       12/22/87                   │
│                                                                          │
│  Forrester      Ridge           Designer       05/07/88                   │
│                                                                          │
│  Jillian        Ross            Salesperson    06/15/90                   │
│ ─────────────────────────────────────────────────────────────────────  │
│  EMPLOYEE.DTF                                                             │
│  ***************************** END OF REPORT ***************************** │
│  Esc-Exit      F2-Reprint      { → ← ↓ ↑ PgUp PgDn }-Scroll   F10-Continue│
└────────────────────────────────────────────────────────────────────────┘
```

Figure 64.1: The Report

Printing a Report with the Query Guide

FEATURING
Printing the report

THE QUERY GUIDE CAN HELP YOU BUILD A REQUEST TO print a predefined report or to print using a predefined print specification. Using Q&A Report you can predefine the terms for a report that you frequently generate. You specify what you always want to include in the report. With a predefined report, you do not have to set up the report each time you want to generate it. Using Q&A File, you can also predefine a specification for printing those records that you want from your database, which also controls how the fields of the record will appear when you print them. This way, you do not have to set up a new print specification every time that you want to print the records in your database.

As stated previously, you don't have to enter any special codes to print the report. Just select the print options from the Query Guide menu and Q&A will print the report based on the requests you make.

Printing a report with the Query Guide is a breeze. There are only two steps: (1) select the Run option and (2) choose the predefined report name from the list displayed on the screen. The predefined reports are the reports you define in the Q&A Report program. The reports print immediately.

*H*ow to Print a Report Using the Query Guide

Let's print the salary report you set up earlier with the Q&A Report program. The predefined salary report will generate a report that shows the salaries for all of the employees at Office Designs.

① To print a report, from the Query Guide menu, press R to select the "Run" option. Then press Enter. The Run menu appears. From here, you can either print a predefined report or print with a print specification.

② From the Query Guide menu, press Enter to select "the report" option.

③ Q&A displays a list of all of the reports predefined for your database. The salary report should appear in your list. Press Enter to select it. Notice that the request "Run the report salary" appears in the Ask box at the top of the screen.

④ Q&A displays a dialog box to ask you if you want to make any temporary changes to the report before printing it.

⑤ Press Enter to select No and continue.

⑥ Q&A displays the message that it will print seven records in your database. Then it prints your salary report.

⑦ Press Esc to exit the Query Guide menu. You are returned to the Assistant menu.

Exiting the Assistant

FEATURING
The Esc key

WHEN YOU HAVE FINISHED BUILDING REQUESTS TO retrieve information from your database, you are ready to exit the Assistant. Let's do that now.

How to Exit the Assistant

To exit the Assistant, press the Esc key. You are returned to the Q&A Main Menu.

PART

SIX

Macros

Recording a Simple Macro

FEATURING

The Shift-F2 Macro function key

MACROS ARE USED TO PERFORM TASKS AUTOMATICALLY that normally would take a long time to do. A macro can store a series of many keystrokes or mouse clicks so that the sequence of commands can be executed automatically with just a few keystrokes. When you use a macro, all you have to do is sit back and watch Q&A do the work.

Some typical macros are used to accomplish the following tasks:

- to create and print letters and memos
- to produce mass mailings
- to print mailing labels
- to retrieve records
- to sort records
- to fill out specs
- to create and print reports
- to create your own menus
- to customize Q&A menus.

When you create a macro in Q&A, there are three guidelines that you should follow. First, study the application that you want to automate and make a plan describing the tasks to be performed by the macro. Second, go through the steps "manually," to make sure that you are familiar with the operations. This means doing *all* of the key-strokes or mouse clicks. If you do not know how to accomplish a task manually, then you will not be able to create a macro to do it. The third and last guideline is to enter the keystrokes or mouse clicks in Q&A to create the macro.

When you create a macro in Q&A, there are four major steps involved: **record**, **define**, **save**, and **run**. You will be exploring all of these steps in the lessons that follow.

You can **record** a macro from anywhere in Q&A. For example, you can record a macro from the Q&A Main Menu, or from Q&A Write, Q&A File, Q&A Report, or the Assistant. You just bring up the Macro menu by pressing the Shift-F2 Macro function key. From the Macro menu you define the macro by assigning a name to it. Then start recording the keystrokes by performing the actions that you want to include in the macro.

*H*ow to Record a Macro

Let's create a simple macro to print the salary report that you created in Part Four, "Q&A Report."

① To record a macro, from the Q&A Main Menu, press the Shift-F2 (Macro) key. Q&A displays the Macro menu, shown in Figure 67.1.

② From the Macro menu, press D to select Define Macro. Then press Enter.

③ A prompt appears at the bottom of the screen asking you to enter a key identifier. (A key identifier can be one key or a combination of keys, such as Alt-A.) However, you will not be entering a key identifier yet, so press Enter now. You will be assigning a descriptive name later to name the macro.

④ Observe the blinking rectangular cursor in the lower right corner of the screen. This indicates that Q&A is in record mode. Remember, every keystroke you enter from this point on is being recorded, just like a tape recorder.

⑤ To start recording, type **R** to select Report and press Enter.

⑥ Type **P** to select Print a report.

⑦ Type **employee** to identify the database file name.

⑧ Press Enter.

⑨ Type **salary** to enter the predefined report name.

⑩ Press Enter to enter the report name Salary.

⑪ Press Enter again to select No to avoid making temporary changes to the report and to print the report.

⑫ Press Esc to exit the Q&A Report menu. This is the last step to record in the macro.

⑬ Press the Shift-F2 (Marco) key to stop recording keystrokes.

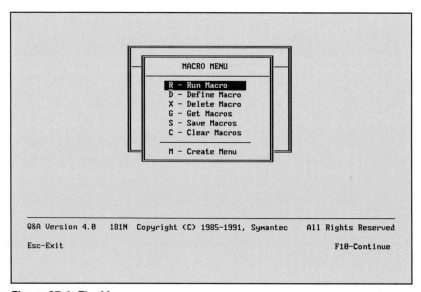

Figure 67.1: *The Macro menu*

Defining and Saving the Macro

FEATURING
Macro options
The Macro file name

THE SECOND STEP FOR CREATING A MACRO IS TO **DEFINE** it. Defining a macro can be done in either of two ways. You can enter a key identifier before you record the macro. A key identifier is one key or a combination of keys, for example, Alt-A, Alt-B. Or, you can assign a descriptive name up to 31-characters long for the macro after the macro has been recorded. For example, "product announcement," and "monthly sales report" are descriptive names.

How to Define a Macro

An appropriate name for your macro would be "salary." Rather than entering a key identifier, let's assign the descriptive name, "salary," to the salary report macro.

① After you tell Q&A to stop recording keystrokes, it displays the Macro Options dialog box, as shown in Figure 68.1.

② Notice the current macro name is "No name #000". Since you did not assign the macro a key identifier earlier, Q&A displays this name instead of a macro name.

LESSON 68

③ To name the macro, type **salary**.

④ Press Enter.

⑤ The Show screen option is set to Yes. This displays menus, screens, and other activities on the screen as the macro plays back. If you choose No, Q&A freezes the screen until the macro finishes playing back. That way, you won't see any action on the screen. Let's leave the option set to Yes.

⑥ Press F10 to save the Macro Options settings.

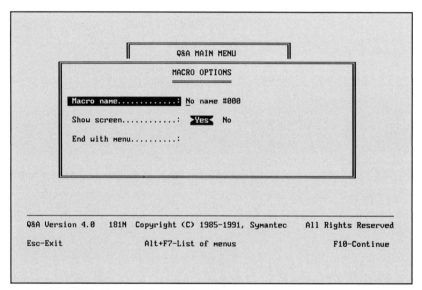

Figure 68.1: *The Macro Options dialog box*

Saving the Macro

Now that you know how to record and define a macro, the third step is to **save** it. All macros are stored in your computer's memory until you exit Q&A. To save a macro and use it again, you must store it with a file name. That way, you can organize your macros by projects, authors, letters, memos, form letters, reports, or Q&A program file names. For example, your word processing macros can be stored with the macro file name "writemac." If you want to store macros by author, use the initials of the author for the macro file name.

When you save a macro for the first time, Q&A will display the file name QAMACRO.ASC. Initially, the QAMACRO.ASC file does not contain macros. You can save your macros by using the QA-MACRO.ASC macro file name which is a convenience. Or, you can type over the QAMACRO.ASC file name and change it to any name you like. That way, you start a new macro file for storing your own macros.

How to Save a Macro

For the purposes of this lesson, let's save the salary report macro in the QAMACRO.ASC macro file. You will learn how to save a macro with a different macro file name later.

1. After you save the Macro Options settings, Q&A displays the macro file name, QAMACRO.ASC.

2. Press Enter to accept it. You have now stored your macro called salary in the QAMACRO.ASC macro file.

Running the Macro

FEATURING

*The Alt-F2 Run Macro function
key*

THE FOURTH AND LAST MAJOR STEP INVOLVED IN CRE-
ating a macro is to **run** it. To run a macro means to play back the keystrokes that were stored in the macro. Q&A lets you run a macro in
any of the four following ways.

- If you assigned a key identifier to your macro, simply press
  the key or keystroke combination that runs the macro.

- If you named the macro with a macro name description,
  you can run the macro from anywhere in Q&A with the
  Shift-F2 (Macro) function key and the Run Macro option.

- You can press the Alt-F2 (Run macro) function key and
  choose the macro name from a list.

- The fourth way to run a macro is to choose a macro from a
  custom menu. Q&A lets you design your own menus that
  will contain menu options to run macros.

Q&A memorizes the last macro file that you worked with. You
can run macros from the current macro file until you want to use
macros from a different macro file. To get a macro file, you must
select the Get Macros option in the Macro menu. Because you stored

your macro in the QAMACRO.ASC file, and you are ready to run it, you won't have to get your macro file. Just run your macro with the Alt-F2 (Run macro) function key, which is a new feature in Q&A Release 4.0.

How to Run a Macro

Let's run the salary report macro with the Alt-F2 (Run macro) function key so that you can see how quickly and easily this new feature works.

① To run the salary report macro from a list, press the Alt-F2 (Run macro) function key. Q&A displays a list of macro names, as shown in Figure 69.1.

② Press Enter to select the macro named "salary."

③ Q&A flashes various commands and menus on the screen as the macro plays back. Within seconds, your salary report prints. You have now run your first macro. To clear the macro out of memory, proceed to the next lesson.

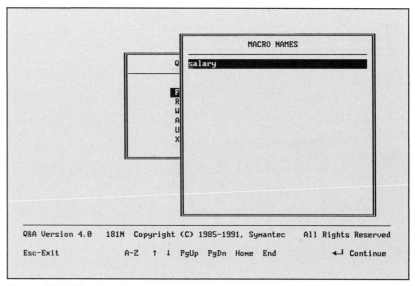

Figure 69.1: *The list of macro names*

LESSON 70

Clearing the Macro

FEATURING
The Shift-F2 Macro function key

THE LAST MACRO FILE YOU WORKED WITH IS STORED IN your computer's memory until you exit Q&A. To clear a macro out of your computer's memory and to use a different macro, you must use the Clear Macros option from the Macro menu. After you clear a macro from memory, you can create a new macro or run a different one.

How to Clear a Macro

To clear the QAMACRO.ASC out of your computer's memory, let's do the following procedures.

1. To clear the macro, press the Shift-F2 (Macro) key to display the Macro menu.

2. From the Macro menu, press C to move the highlight to the Clear Macros option.

3. Press Enter. Q&A immediately clears the macro without a warning message. The QAMACRO.ASC macro file is no longer in your computer's memory.

If you want to take a break now, this is a good place to stop. You are at the Q&A Main Menu. If you want to further explore creating macros, proceed to the next lesson on Creating a Word Processing Macro.

Creating a Word Processing Macro

___

FEATURING

The Shift-F2 Macro function key
The Alt-F2 Run Macro function key

SUPPOSE THAT YOU WANT THE COMPANY NAME OF Office Designs to appear at the top of every piece of correspondence written in Q&A Write. You can create a macro to do just that. Each time you create a document, you can add a header to the document with a macro instead of having to enter the header information with the Edit Header option.

How to Create a Word Processing Macro

Let's start Q&A Write, create a new document, and then create the macro. We will start recording the macro from the Type/Edit screen in Q&A Write.

1. From the Q&A Main Menu, press W and then press Enter to load Q&A Write into your computer's memory.

2. From the Q&A Write menu, press Enter to select the Type/Edit option.

3. To create the macro, press the Shift-F2 (Macro) key. Q&A displays the Macro menu.

④ From the Macro menu, press D to select Define Macro. Then press Enter.

⑤ Press Enter again. This skips the task of assigning a key indentifier to the macro. You will define the macro later.

⑥ To record the keystrokes for creating header information, press F8 to display the Options menu.

⑦ Press the Right-Arrow key to move the highlight to the submenu.

⑧ Press Enter to select the Edit Header option.

⑨ Type **Office Designs** and press Enter.

⑩ Press F10 to exit the Header window and return to your document. This is the last step to record in the macro.

⑪ Press the Shift-F2 (Macro) key to stop recording keystrokes.

Defining and Saving the Word Processing Macro

An appropriate name for your macro would be "header." After you define the macro, you can save it in a new macro file. Because the header macro is a word processing macro, an appropriate name for the macro file name would be "writemac."

How to Define a Macro

Let's assign the descriptive name, "header," to the macro.

① After you tell Q&A to stop recording keystrokes, Q&A displays the Macro Options dialog box.

② Type over "No name #000" with the name **header**.

③ Press Enter.

④ Press F10 to save the Macro Options settings.

⑤ Type over QAMACRO.ASC with the name **writemac** and press Enter. You have now stored your header macro in a new macro file called WRITEMAC.

Running the Word Processing Macro

Let's play back the keystrokes that you stored in the header macro with the Alt-F2 (Run macro) function key. This will enter the header "Office Designs" on every page of a document.

How to Run the Word Processing Macro

First, let's clear the current document because it already contains the header, "Office Designs." When you clear the Type/Edit screen, Q&A will create a new document. Then, you can run the word processing macro and add the header to the top of each page in the new document.

① Press Esc to exit the Type/Edit screen.

② From the Q&A Write menu, press C to select the Clear option.

③ Press Enter to select the Clear option.

④ Q&A asks you if you want to lose the changes you made to the current document. Press the Left-Arrow key to select Yes. Then press Enter. This clears the Type/Edit screen.

⑤ The message "New document" appears at the bottom of the screen. Now you are ready to run the macro in the new document.

⑥ To run the header macro from a list, press the Alt-F2 (Run macro) function key. Q&A displays a list of macro names.

⑦ Move the highlight to the macro named "header" and press Enter.

⑧ Q&A flashes various commands and menus on the screen as the macro plays back. Within seconds, the header information is added to the top of page 1 in your document.

⑨ Using the PgDn key, move the cursor down through the document to view the header information on each page.

⑩ After you finish looking at the header information in your document, you can clear the macro file out of your computer's memory. Press the Shift-F2 (Macro) key to display the Macro menu.

⑪ Press C to select Clear Macros and then press Enter. Q&A immediately clears the macro without a warning message.

⑫ To exit Q&A Write, press Esc to exit the Type/Edit screen. Press Esc again to exit Q&A Write. Q&A Write asks you if you want to lose the changes you made to the current document. Press the Left-Arrow key to select Yes. Then press Enter. This exits Q&A Write and you are returned to the Q&A Main Menu.

If you want to take a break now, this is a good place to stop. You are at the Q&A Main Menu. If you want to further explore creating macros, proceed to the next lesson on Creating a Macro to Back Up a Document.

Creating a Macro to Back Up a Document

FEATURING

The Shift-F2 Macro function key
The WRITEMAC macro file

YOU SHOULD BACK UP DOCUMENTS TO A FLOPPY DISK
frequently to ensure their safety. There are many steps involved when
backing up a document to a floppy disk, as discussed earlier in Lesson
31, "Copying a Document: Backing Up the Document to a Floppy
Disk." Instead of performing the keystrokes every time you back up a
document, you can use a macro to do it.

How to Create a Macro to Back Up a Document

Let's start Q&A Write and create the macro. We will start recording the macro from the Q&A Write menu.

1. Insert a formatted floppy disk in Drive A.

2. From the Q&A Main Menu, press W and then press Enter to
   load Q&A Write into your computer's memory.

3. To create the macro, press the Shift-F2 (Macro) key. Q&A
   displays the Macro menu.

④ From the Macro menu, press D to select Define Macro. Then press Enter.

⑤ Press Enter again. This skips the task of assigning a key indentifier to the macro. You will define the macro later.

⑥ To record the keystrokes for copying the KASELTR1 file to a floppy disk, press U to move the highlight to the Utilities option. Then press Enter.

⑦ Press D to move the highlight to the DOS facilities option. Then press Enter.

⑧ Press C to select the Copy a document option. Q&A prompts you to enter the name of the database you want to copy.

⑨ Type **kaseltr1** and press Enter. This tells Q&A Write which document you want to copy from the hard disk to the floppy disk.

⑩ Press the Backspace key six times to erase C:\QA\.

⑪ Type **a:\kaseltr1** and press Enter. This tells Q&A Write that you want to copy the KASELTR1 file to the floppy disk in Drive A. Q&A copies the file to the floppy disk in Drive A.

⑫ Press Esc twice to exit the Q&A Utilities menu and to return to the Q&A Write menu. This is the last step to record in the macro.

⑬ Press the Shift-F2 (Macro) key to stop recording keystrokes.

Defining and Saving the Macro

An appropriate name for your macro would be "backup." After you define the word processing macro, you can save the macro in the WRITEMAC macro file.

*H*ow to Define the Macro

Let's assign the descriptive name, "backup," to the macro.

① After you tell Q&A to stop recording keystrokes, Q&A displays the Macro Options dialog box.

② Type over "No name #000" with the name **backup**.

③ Press Enter.

④ Press F10 to save the Macro Options settings.

⑤ The macro file name **writemac** appears in the dialog box. Press Enter to accept it. You have now stored your header macro in the macro file called WRITEMAC.

Let's play back the keystrokes you stored in the backup macro with the Alt-F2 (Run macro) function key.

*H*ow to Run the Word Processing Macro

We will run the word processing backup macro to back up the KASELTR1 file to a floppy disk.

① To run the header macro from a list, press the Alt-F2 (Run macro) function key. Q&A displays a list of macro names.

② Move the highlight to the macro named "backup" and press Enter.

③ Q&A flashes various commands and menus on the screen as the macro plays back. Within seconds, the KASELTR1 file is copied to the floppy disk in Drive A.

④ Remove the diskette from Drive A.

⑤ Press C to select the Clear Macros option and then press Enter. Q&A immediately clears the macro without a warning message.

⑥ Press Esc to exit Q&A Write. You are returned to the Q&A Main Menu.

When you have completed the steps above and you are secure with your knowledge about how to create macros in Q&A, then you can begin creating your own macros and saving yourself time and keystrokes.

Installation

Preparing Data Disks

If you plan to copy information from your hard disk onto a diskette for use on another computer or to back up the files that you create in Q&A, you will have to format some floppy disks.

This lesson assumes that you have a hard-disk system with one or two floppy disk drives. Keep in mind, too, that there are different density capacities for floppy disks and floppy drives. If the densities of your drive and disks do not match, see your DOS manual.

How to Prepare Blank Disks

Let's format two floppy disks with the DOS FORMAT command to prepare them for use.

① Turn on your computer.

② After DOS loads into your computer's memory, you should see the C:\> prompt on your screen.

③ Type **format a:** and press Enter.

④ DOS prompts you to insert a disk into drive A.

⑤ Insert an unformatted disk into drive A.

⑥ Press Enter to start formatting the disk.

⑦ When DOS finishes formatting your disk, it asks you if you want to format another disk.

⑧ Type **Y** for Yes.

⑨ Replace the formatted disk in drive **A** with the second unformatted disk.

⑩ Press Enter to format the second disk.

⑪ After you have finished formatting the second disk, type **N** for No, to end the formatting process. The C:\> prompt reappears on the screen.

⑫ Put blank labels on the diskettes. Later, when you write on the disk labels, remember to use a felt-tip pen. Metal-tipped pens, such as ball-points, can harm floppy disks.

Upgrading Your PC

If you are upgrading from an earlier version of Q&A, you can also follow the steps provided below. Be sure to back up any files that you created with an earlier version of Q&A. Since the printer settings information is lost during the upgrade of Q&A 4.0., be sure to make a note of the types of printers you had installed and any other relevant printer information. Keep in mind the fact that once a database is upgraded in Q&A 4.0, you cannot use it with an earlier version of Q&A. You still can use your QAMACRO.ASC macro file in Q&A 4.0; however, some of the menus have changed, so you might have to redefine some macros to run them.

How to Install Q&A

Q&A Release 4.0 can be run only from your hard disk. The program does not work on systems with two floppy disk drives and no hard disk.

Installing Q&A on your hard disk takes about 20 minutes. Be sure that you have the time to finish before you start the installation. If you turn off your computer during installation, you can experience difficulty installing the program.

Q&A comes with seven 5-1/4-inch floppy disks labeled #1 through #7 and four 3-1/2-inch floppy disks labeled #1 through #4.

These disks include an Install program that automatically installs Q&A onto your hard disk.

After taking all of the floppy disks that come with Q&A out of the package, you're ready to install Q&A.

① To write-protect your Q&A program disks, we recommend that you place a gummed write-protect tab over the small rectangular slot cut in on the right side of each 5-1/4-inch diskette. If you use 3-1/2-inch diskettes, slide the write-protect tab up. This tab is on the back of the diskette in the upper-left corner. The write-protect tab protects the disk from being accidentally erased, and it allows you to copy information from the diskette. To store new information on the diskette, you would have to remove the tab on the 5-1/4-inch diskette, or slide the write-protect tab down on the 3-1/2-inch diskette. Write-protect tabs come with your Q&A disks and are included in boxes of new blank diskettes.

② If your computer is not turned on, then turn it on now. You should see the C:\> prompt on your screen.

③ Insert the Q&A #1 install disk in drive A.

④ Type **a:** and press Enter.

⑤ Type **install** and press Enter.

⑥ In a few seconds, you are presented with the Install program screen. Press Enter to continue.

⑦ Q&A asks you for the name of the source drive. This is the drive from which you are copying the files. A: should be highlighted. If A: is not highlighted, press the Up-Arrow key to highlight it. Then press Enter.

⑧ Q&A asks you for the name of the destination drive. This is the drive to which you are copying the files. Notice that A: is highlighted. You will install Q&A on the hard disk, which is usually the C:drive. Press the Down-Arrow key to highlight C: and then press Enter.

⑨ Q&A scans drive C for any copies of Q&A. If Q&A doesn't find any copies of the program, it displays the pathname C:\QA. The pathname contains the letter C which is the name of the hard disk and the directory name QA which is where you will install the Q&A program.

⑩ Press Enter to accept it.

⑪ If you are upgrading from an earlier version of Q&A, the Install program will find the existing copy of Q&A. Then you can choose to overwrite the existing copy or to copy Q&A to a new directory. If you want to overwrite the existing copy of Q&A, Q&A gives you the option to make a backup copy of it.

⑫ Press Enter to select Complete Installation. If you want to install only the additional program files, select Partial Installation.

⑬ Q&A copies the information on the first install disk to your hard disk. Observe the bars that appear in the middle of the screen. These are called progress bars that show you the progress of the installation. When it finishes, you are prompted to insert disk #2.

⑭ Put disk #2 in drive A and press Enter.

⑮ Repeat Steps 13 and 14 until you see the message "Installation of Program Files Successfully completed" on your screen.

⑯ When the Install program finishes copying the Q&A program files to your hard disk, press Enter. You are prompted to install additional Q&A program files. We recommend that you go through the rest of the installation procedure because there might be some additional program files that can be useful to you when you are working with Q&A. For instructions on installing these files, proceed to the next section.

If you want to exit the Install program, you can press Ctrl-Q or Esc at any time. Depending on where you are in the Install program, Q&A will prompt you to press either of these keys to exit.

Installing Additional Q&A Program Files

You can install additional Q&A program files after you install the basic Q&A program files on your hard disk. The additional files include font description files, ready-to-use database files, and additional Q&A utilities.

The font description files tell your printer how to print with fonts. For example, if you print with various fonts such as fonts on cartridges, or soft fonts on a Hewlett-Packard LaserJet or PostScript laser printer, then you must install the appropriate font files for your printer.

The ready-to-use database files are files that you can use with the Q&A tutorial to learn Q&A. The additional utilities include several files that allow you to perform special operations. For example, QABACKUP.EXE lets you back up database files larger than the size of one floppy disk. HIMEM.SYS lets you increase the amount of memory available to Q&A, if you have extended memory. Extended memory is memory above 640K. QAFONT.EXE allows you to upgrade a font description file from an earlier version of Q&A. It also lets you add soft font or PostScript printer files to your font description files.

You can also ask Q&A to modify your CONFIG.SYS file so that your computer can handle the files you create in Q&A.

How to Install Additional Program Files

When you install each set of additional program files, Q&A asks you if you want to install the files. If you want to continue the installation, Q&A will display a list of the files. You select the files you want to install and then enter a directory name for each set of files. Q&A will prompt you to insert another disk when necessary. When you install all of the additional program files, you should use all of the install disks provided by Symantec. You can stop the installation procedure at any time by pressing Esc or Ctrl-Q, whichever key is noted at the bottom of the screen. Let's see how you can install these program files and modify the CONFIG.SYS file.

1. Q&A asks you if you want to install the font files. Press Enter.

2. Q&A displays a list of font files. Using the Down-Arrow and Up-Arrow keys, move the highlighted bar to the printer for which you want to install fonts.

3. Press the Spacebar to tag the file. A checkmark displays to the left of the font file. If you have more than one printer for which you want to install fonts, repeat Steps 3 and 4 to select additional font files. If you want to select all of the font files, press F5. To untag a font file (this removes the checkmark), press the Spacebar.

4. Press Enter. Q&A prompts you to enter a name for the font directory.

5. Fonts is an appropriate directory name. Type **fonts** and press Enter.

6. Q&A installs the font description files. Press Enter.

7. Q&A asks if you want to install the tutorial files. Press Enter to continue.

8. Q&A displays a list of the tutorial files. To select all of the files, press F5. Notice a checkmark appears to the left of each tutorial file.

9. Press Enter. Q&A prompts you to enter a directory name.

10. Tutor is an appropriate name for the tutorial files directory. Type **tutor** and press Enter.

11. Q&A installs the tutorial files. Press Enter.

12. To install the rest of the additional program files, repeat Steps 2 through 9. You can use the directory names, "readyfil," for the ready-to-use files and "util" for the utilities files.

⑬ After you install the additional program files, press Enter. Q&A asks you to modify the CONFIG.SYS file. Press Enter to change it. If no changes are necessary, Q&A will display a message telling you that no changes were required. Otherwise, Q&A will automatically update your CONFIG.SYS file so that your computer can handle the files you create in Q&A.

⑭ Press Enter twice to exit the Install program and return to DOS. The A:\> prompt appears on your screen.

⑮ Remove the last install disk from the disk drive. You have now completed the installation of Q&A and updated your CONFIG.SYS file.

⑯ Type **C:** and press Enter. There are two more installation procedures that you must perform before working with the Q&A program: setting up your monitor and setting up your printer. Proceed to the next section for instructions on how to do these tasks.

Setting Up Your Monitor

Q&A is influenced by the kind of equipment on which it operates. For example, Q&A needs to know what kind of display screen or monitor you are using. Are you operating a black-and-white (monochrome) or a color display monitor?

If you are using any other type of monitor, refer to the Q&A documentation for a list of other monitors and instructions on how to start Q&A with your type of monitor.

Let's set up your monitor and tell Q&A what kind of display you are using.

① To change to the Q&A directory, from the C drive, type **cd\qa** and press Enter.

② If you have a monochrome monitor, type **qa -smc -a**. Be sure to type a space before each dash. If you don't, the monitor setting will not work. If that isn't successful, type **qa -smm**. If you have a color monitor, type **qa -scc**.

③ Press Enter. This sets up your monitor and starts the program.

④ Your screen should appear either in black and white, or in color, depending on the type of monitor you are using. You only have to start Q&A with the extra characters once. After you start Q&A for the first time, you can simply enter QA each time you start the program.

Setting Up Your Printer

Q&A also needs to know what kind of printer you are using. For example, are you working with an Epson LQ1500 dot-matrix printer or a Hewlett-Packard LaserJet Series II printer?

Let's step through setting up your printer for use with Q&A.

① The first time you start Q&A, you will see a message at the bottom of the screen that reminds you to use the Utilities option to set up your printer.

② From the Q&A Main Menu, press U to select Utilities and then press Enter.

③ Press Enter to select Install Printer. Q&A displays the Printer Selection screen.

④ The first printer, Printer A, is already highlighted. Press Enter to select it.

⑤ Q&A displays the Port Selection screen. Using the Up-Arrow and Down-Arrow keys, select one of the ports. LPT1 is the port option usually used for most printers. An LPT option is for a parallel printer and a COM option is for a serial printer. If you don't know whether your printer is parallel or serial, refer to your printer manual or ask your computer dealer. Press Enter to select LPT1.

⑥ Q&A displays a list of printer manufacturers. Using the arrow keys and the PgDn key, select the manufacturer of your printer and press Enter.

⑦ Q&A displays a list of printer models. Using the arrow keys and the PgDn key, select the model of your printer and press Enter.

⑧ Q&A displays information about your printer's capabilities. Press Enter again to confirm installing your printer.

⑨ Q&A asks you if you want to install another printer. If you don't, press Enter to select No. If you want to install another printer, press the Left-Arrow key to choose Yes, and then press Enter. Then repeat Steps 3 through 8 in this lesson.

⑩ Press Esc to exit the Utilities menu. You are returned to the Q&A Main Menu. Now you are ready to work with Q&A.

INDEX

maximum columns in reports, 149
maximum reports per database, 144
Speed up searches option, 107
Spelling Checker, 52–56
Spelling menu, 52–53
square brackets ([ ]), 62, 65–66
starting, 5
    Assistant, 176–177
    File (Q&A), 87–88
    Report (Q&A), 146
    Write (Q&A), 16–17
Status line
    in File (Q&A), 91
    in Write (Q&A), 18, 29–30
strikeouts, 59
subscripts, 59
superscripts, 59

T

T (tab). *See* tabs
T (text) information type, 102
T (total) code, 155
Tab key, 67–68
Tab menu, 63, 64
Table (Alt-F6) function key, 124
Table view feature (Alt-F6), 120–122
tabs
    for columns, 62
    creating, 18
    for indenting, 67–68
    removing, 65
    setting, 62–65
Teach me about your database option, 176
Teach Query Guide option, 176, 178–180
Teach Query Guide Spec, 179
telephone numbers template, 107–108
text
    centering, 68–69
    copying, 43–44
    correcting, 34–35
    deleting, 38–40
    indenting, 67–68
    inserting, 36–37
    inserting page breaks in, 70–71
    moving, 45–46
    replacing, 49–51
    restoring, 41–42
    searching for, 47–48

Text Enhancements and Fonts menu, 60–61, 158–160
Text feature for database retrieval, 116
Thesaurus, 57–58
Thesaurus (Alt-F1) function key, 57–58
Time feature for range retrieval, 115
title pages, 72
total code (T), 155
total label (TL) code, 156–157
Tutorial installation, 219
Type of Paper Feed option, 79
Type/Edit option, 16, 18–19

U

underlining, 59–61
undo, 41–42
Up-Arrow key, 30, 32
Update option, 120–122
updating of forms, 120–122
upgrading Q&A, 215, 217
uppercase characters, 48, 106
Utilities option, 17, 81–83, 87
    accessing, 7
    additional, 218
    for printer set up, 221–222

V

viewing. *See* previewing

W

word processing macro
    clearing, 209
    creating, 206–207
    defining, 207–208
    naming, 207
    running, 208–209
word wrapping, 20, 67
words
    deleting, 38–39
    moving cursor left and right, 31
    restoring deleted, 41–42
    Search/Replace, 49–51
    searching for, 47–48
    spell checking, 52–56
working copy, 18, 24

SYBEX®

FREE CATALOG!

Mail us this form today, and we'll send you a full-color catalog of Sybex books.

Name _____

Street _____

City/State/Zip _____

Phone _____

Please supply the name of the Sybex book purchased.

_____

How would you rate it?

_____ Excellent   _____ Very Good   _____ Average   _____ Poor

Why did you select this particular book?

_____ Recommended to me by a friend

_____ Recommended to me by store personnel

_____ Saw an advertisement in _____

_____ Author's reputation

_____ Saw in Sybex catalog

_____ Required textbook

_____ Sybex reputation

_____ Read book review in _____

_____ In-store display

_____ Other _____

Where did you buy it?

_____ Bookstore

_____ Computer Store or Software Store

_____ Catalog (name: _____)

_____ Direct from Sybex

_____ Other: _____

Did you buy this book with your personal funds?

_____ Yes   _____ No

About how many computer books do you buy each year?

_____ 1-3   _____ 3-5   _____ 5-7   _____ 7-9   _____ 10+

About how many Sybex books do you own?

_____ 1-3   _____ 3-5   _____ 5-7   _____ 7-9   _____ 10+

Please indicate your level of experience with the software covered in this book:

_____ Beginner   _____ Intermediate   _____ Advanced

Which types of software packages do you use regularly?

_____ Accounting   _____ Databases   _____ Networks

_____ Amiga   _____ Desktop Publishing   _____ Operating Systems

_____ Apple/Mac   _____ File Utilities   _____ Spreadsheets

_____ CAD   _____ Money Management   _____ Word Processing

_____ Communications   _____ Languages   _____ Other _____

(please specify)

Which of the following best describes your job title?

_____ Administrative/Secretarial   _____ President/CEO

_____ Director   _____ Manager/Supervisor

_____ Engineer/Technician   _____ Other _____

(please specify)

Comments on the weaknesses/strengths of this book: _____

_____

_____

_____

_____

PLEASE FOLD, SEAL, AND MAIL TO SYBEX

– –

SYBEX, INC.
Department M
2021 CHALLENGER DR.
ALAMEDA, CALIFORNIA USA
94501

SYBEX ®

SEAL

Q&A Report

MENU SELECTION	DESCRIPTION
Design/Redesign a report	Creates columnar and cross-tab reports
Print a report	Prints reports
Set global options	Sets formatting and printing options
Rename/Delete/Copy	Renames, deletes, and copies report files

Q&A Write

MENU SELECTION	DESCRIPTION
Type/Edit	Creates a document and a mail merge document
Define page	Defines page size for a document, *i.e.*, margins and page length
Print	Prints a document
Clear	Removes a document from memory
Get	Retrieves a document
Save	Saves a document
Utilities	Imports/exports documents, recovers damaged documents, sets global formatting options
Mailing Labels	Creates mailing labels